AFFORDABLE COUTURE

A guide to buying and collecting

AFFORDABLE COUTURE

Jemi Armstrong
Linda Arroz

VIVAYS PUBLISHING

Published by Vivays Publishing
www.vivays-publishing.com

A catalogue record for this book is available from the British Library

ISBN 978-1-908126-24-5

Publishing Director: Lee Ripley
Design Concept: Price Watkins
Design: Tiziana Lardieri

Printed in China

Contents

Introduction

Beautiful clothing inhabits a mythical place in our minds. It can bring the wearer iconic status, forever linking the clothes to a time, place, lifestyle, film, or bygone era. Close your eyes and think *Breakfast at Tiffany's* or *Designing Women*. The first image that springs to mind is of a svelte woman impeccably tailored, narrow hipped, pelvis thrust forward, long cigarette holder in hand... the glamour is palpable. Audrey Hepburn and Lauren Bacall are stunning women in their own right; however, they are forever linked to Hubert Givenchy, Helen Rose, and the transcendently chic period of the 1950s and early 60s. This sophisticated mystique is why we covet glamorous items of legendary status. Collecting couture is a way to obtain – via beautiful clothing – the panache created by these women. Through osmosis we feel the chic style and confidence of a Hepburn and Bacall; it can be ours momentarily, but immortality is possible through great fabric and great design – whether couture or ready-to-wear.

Shopping isn't the only way to lose oneself in the pursuit of couture. Museums around the world spotlight the art and legacy of their couture designers via their gallery exhibitions space, by international traveling exhibitions, and virtual tours of their fashion collections, while auction houses present couture as art for bidding, and fittingly so.

Shopping is not the destination: it is the journey. When investigating vintage or resale or newly reduced, remember that there is never a wasted visit; you are educating yourself by visually absorbing the taste level of each store buyer when you enter the shop or click on their website or blog. When shopping for *yourself* (not rushing to find something for a last-minute event), you are truly "building" your personal wardrobe. Success is when one can say, "I don't need any more clothing," but bliss is constantly exploring and adding the spices to an already secure selection. Your inspiration may come from a museum, a magazine, a film, a store, or a mirror, and we hope this book will help to guide you in creating a wonderful collection that you will love for years to come.

That was then,
this is now

01

That was then, this is now

Am I a fool when I dream of putting art into my dresses, a fool when I say dressmaking is an art?
Paul Poiret (My First Fifty Years)

"Couture represents the fusion of fashion—the modern entity that combines novelty and synergy with personal and social needs and costume—the arts of dressmaking, tailoring, and crafts constituent to apparel and accessories." So said Harold Koda, director at the Costume Institute of the Metropolitan Museum of Art in a 2004 essay on haute couture.

Is it fashion or fine art?

At the turn of the 20th century commerce collided with an artisan world. This collision accounts for a lot of the conflict and brilliance created in the pre and post World Wars. Advances in technology and industrialization made art, or some version of it, available on a grand scale to more than just wealthy patrons. From this period onward one can perceive fashion as a metaphor useful in gaining a larger understanding of a world being impacted by mass production. Replacing original handcrafted items with an industrial economy has inherent anxiety that transforms society in far-reaching ways.

In the history of fashion and design, a great idea typically spawned a unique item to be possessed by someone rich enough to

own it. Now the same design could be translated into a template for a product that could be reproduced and possessed by thousands of people of relatively modest means. The sudden competitive friction of art-meets-commerce led to a period of artistic innovation that we still celebrate today.

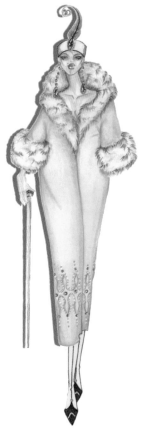

Muse Denise Poiret popularized the opera style coat in 1911. Many of the styles photographed on Madam Poiret and published in fashion magazines were conceived for the leading actresses of the day. This practice allowed Paul Poiret to indulge his more theatrical impulses and design at intersections where art, theater, and fashion collide.

Beginning in the 1930s drop waist slip dresses with lavish beading were popularized by French designers Lanvin, Chanel and Vionnet. Women were encouraged to apply Vaseline "gloss" to their eyelids and speak in monosyllabic slang. These practices prompted a journalist to write, "We are in an abbreviated period – short skirts, short shrift, short credit, and short names."

Paul Poiret's new less expensive versions of his couture garments were labeled with the fabulous oxymoron "genuine reproductions"; it was one man's attempt to cope with an increasingly complex world. In turn, Poiret's luxurious, ornate, exotic gowns, which had seemed so perfect for the early part of the century, would be replaced by Coco Chanel's chic, liberating "garçonne" look. Chanel's suits were dubbed the "Ford" of designer styles, after Henry Ford, the inventor of the assembly line. But the fashion fit the times as women were being swept into the future and wanted simplicity and functionality. Chanel's clothing was decidedly masculine and appeared appropriate and chic after the sobering experiences of the First World War. Women, fashion, and technology in the post-war world would take a decided march forward as part of a modern consumer commodity culture.

"I don't make art I make clothes," exclaimed Jean Paul Gaultier. Most would dispute that comment. JPG's glittering Les Vierges (virgins) collection from Spring/Summer 2007 Haute Couture does what all great art aspires to do; combine the familiar with the unexpected. This formula of juxtaposing outrageous controversial elements creates epic results. Jean Paul Gaultier has the reputation of being an enfant terrible; perhaps it is time to add "genius" to that phrase.

Chanel's suits were dubbed the "Ford" of designer styles

Designer to demi-god

Prior to the late 19th and early 20th centuries, couturiers were relatively unknown and generally worked in the service of aristocrats. The very necessity of extensive manual labor (which these garments required) robbed the artist and clothing of its rightful place as an aesthetic art. Ornate dressmaking was a very utilitarian business. A laborer sewing on rows of pearls for weeks on end does not smack of artistry, it smacks of the mundane. This laborious sewing of early couture pieces relegated even the creation of spectacular garments to the arena of "craft." Works of art in the traditional media (sculpture, painting or architecture) were perceived as somehow apart from the creator, not a product of human creativity as much as something inspired by God. This attitude of elevating artwork to the divine did not allow for the skill, drudgery and trial and error that so often applied to making fine garments. It just didn't measure up as *art*.

Noted fashion historian and educator Lorrie Ivas feels there is a legitimate connoisseurship of couture garments. The functionality of clothing does not negate its value, as some traditional art critics would have one believe. Lorrie stated, "Ever since Diana Vreeland and Tiffany Dubin brought their trained and refined sense of style to the Metropolitan Museum of Art's Costume Institute and Sotheby's, respectively, they exposed the general public to couture as an art form. Couture clothing has been elevated to the elite status of fine art."

Today we understand the creative process intellectually; however, the artist as genius myth still persists, with all its misconceptions and subtle forms of prejudice. It is hard to reconcile the mythological artist with the pragmatic dressmaker. Perhaps that is why it has taken so long for couture garments to be recognized as an art form worthy of museum conservation. Or perhaps it is the transient and degradable nature of textiles. How many glorious creations have simply dissolved with the passing of time?

One suspects the dilemma that clothing faces simply has more to do with the nature of clothing – part art, part craft and all the variations in between. This dilemma leads us to repeatedly categorize fashion as more functional than artistic. It is with the perspective of time that we are able to appreciate the true nature, value and beauty of, for example, an early Worth gown. The craftsmanship and elegance of such a garment are obvious and certainly qualify it as an art piece.

Cristobal Balenciaga designed the bubble cocktail dress in 1958. The bubble silhouette made a comeback in 2007. Balenciaga was considered a prophet for his innovations and impeccable techniques.

Defining historic couture

The Chambre syndicale de la haute couture was created in 1868. The French Federation comprises three separate entities:

- **Chambre Syndicale de la Haute Couture** a trade union of high fashion or "haute couture"
- **Chambre Syndicale de la Mode Masculine** a trade union of men's ready-to-wear fashion – created in 1973
- **Chambre Syndicale du Prêt-à-Porter des Couturiers et des Créateurs de Mode** a trade union of women's ready-to-wear of couturiers and fashion designers – created in 1973

The Federation also has a fashion school, the **École de la Chambre Syndicale de la Couture Parisienne** created in 1928. The French organization was established to control, promote and publicize French fashion houses. The Federation is responsible for setting the dates and location of the French fashion weeks. It also establishes industry standards on quality and on the use of the word *haute couture*.

Cinema Satin long dress circa 1931 designed by Alix (who later became known as Madam Grès) coined the term "sheath" to describe the gown. *Vogue* would claim that the fit has a poured in appearance. Fashion editors wrote that women can and should "show the body as a superb piece of sculpture."

The early fashion houses of Worth, Vionnet, Patou, Lanvin, and Poiret created original, custom, hand-sewn garments for wealthy clients. Haute couture garments were specifically made to fit the individual client and sewn out of luxurious fabrics directly on the client. Intricate costly trims and beading applied to unique garments

1947 Christian Dior New Look suit was originally dubbed "The Bar Suit." Look for affordable versions of this suit in select resale stores.

required hundreds of hours to create. Charles Fredrick Worth is considered the father of haute couture. However, it was Paul Poiret who first discovered what would eventually be classified as the "lifestyle" market with infinite opportunities for consumers to own a small piece of luxury. If a woman could not own a garment by the designer, she could have a modified version or a decorative art item. Haute couture was always defined by the Chambre Syndicale as the art of dressmaking elevated to its utmost expression. Today the very word "couture" is in dispute. Couture can mean something different in every country and varies from designer to designer. Haute couture has a rigid set of standards to which the members of the elite Chambre Syndicale de la Haute Couture are required to adhere. The couture house is composed of two sections: the dressmaking section and the tailoring section, which creates the suits and coats. Skilled workers practice the art of couture side by side with constant supervision of the designers and *vendeuses*. Embellishment, beading and decorative elements are added incrementally to the garment.

Depending upon the house, the process begins with sketches or with lengths of muslin, draped and cut. Next the garment is fitted, and a trusted fitter will conduct the client through a series of fittings to determine the smallest adjustments of the piece. This is inevitably part of the value and virtue of the couture model.

If a woman could not own a garment by the designer, she could have a modified version or a decorative art item.

The French Federation still describes garments that meet the Chambre Syndicale standards as haute couture fashion. Many designers today have less strict definitions of what couture is. The definition is sometimes used to describe garments that are custom-made, expensive, unique and one of a kind, but this does not necessarily mean it is a couture garment. The word "couture" has obviously taken on multiple and sometimes nebulous meaning. Couture in the purest use of the word is an art form, created by highly skilled craftsmen and women and requires long years of dedication and training in an apprentice system.

André Courrèges designed some of the most memorable mini-dresses of the 1960s. Courrèges trained with Balenciaga and his sense of proportion was masterful. He stressed accessories with his mini-dress creations for correct proportions and balance and to remain in contact with the earth and reality.

2012 LIST CHAMBRE SYNDICALE DE LA HAUTE COUTURE

- Adeline André
- Atelier Gustavolins
- Chanel
- Christian Dior
- Christophe Josse
- Anne Valérie Hash

- Maurizio Galante
- Jean Paul Gaultier
- Givenchy
- Stéphane Rolland
- Franck Sorbier
- Giambattista Valli

Frocks of fantasy

Designers need to be part Coco Chanel and part PT Barnum. Today's celebrity culture has fueled an elaborate network of sub-celebrity worlds. This orbit extends to those who contribute and function in the glamour universe even in peripheral ways. Elaborate and expensive runway shows are big publicity opportunities. They are also viewed as a kind of laboratory for experimentation; the stakes must constantly be raised and reinvented, turning fashion into performance art. The celebrities, clients, and fashion editors who attend these extravagant runway shows as well as the general public who follow them via the Internet now have instant access in real time. This requires constant razzle-dazzle on an epic scale. Designers seize the opportunity to captivate the world through outrageous displays of mind-boggling combinations of fabric and fantasy. Not all designers preview their latest collections as runway spectacle, however. Generally Italian designers and most New York houses favor function over fantasy. The fantasy garments that come down the runway are not intended to be

Extreme couture garments or fantasy couture have a "flash bulb" effect. These runway creations can be both dramatic and experimental. Inspiration for these magnificent pieces can be derived from a wide variety of influences including; historical icons, cultural concepts, or art movements.

functional. These fantasy garments are experimental, promotional, and outrageous for outrage's sake. They should not be viewed as anything else. It is sometimes hard for the general public to grasp these subtle concepts and so the result is a misunderstanding of designer and couture fashion.

After the runway shows that preview the latest collection and showcase a designer's point of view for that particular season, a separate collection is created. This secondary collection or *prêt-à-porter* line is the group of garments intended for a limited mass production to the general public. These garments will end up in department stores and specialty boutiques. As the quality of construction and fabrication gets reinterpreted the market gets less exclusive and the prices generally drop. This is the basic economic model. However, in more recent times the speed at which high fashion gets reinterpreted or "knocked-off" is lightening fast. It is estimated that the wedding dress worn by Kate Middleton, the future Queen of England, was reproduced and ready for delivery from Chinese factories within one week to ten days of its airing on global television. This is the "Paris to Peoria effect."

A simple yet elegant polka-dot Valentino gown from the 1980s. This piece shows the international couturier's art. "The French are fortunate to have Valentino" remarked the *International Herald Tribune*.

During the 30s and 40s
Hollywood starlets and
their costume designers
set the trends that
women emulated. Jean
Louis designed the
famous "Gilda" dress for
Rita Hayworth. The
dress was an instant hit.
Similarly Adrian's "Letty
Lynton" 1932 dress
designed for Joan
Crawford was copied by
Macys department store
and sold over 500,000
dresses nationwide.

The Masonic handshake

Wearing an understated, dramatic, paradoxically sophisticated Issey Miyake jacket speaks volumes about a woman. The Miyake jacket commands respect from other women in the know. It's a form of secret knowledge – only for the initiated. This coded clothing says, "I am one of the coastal or international intelligent set." It defines income, sophistication, taste, and that intangible commodity known as social status. It's much like the secret handshakes used by medieval stone masons traveling from village to village; it identified a fellow mason and therefore someone who was "one of us" and worthy of wages and lodging. Couture garments today are still a form of

Signature origami pleating in Issey Miyake's work is both understated and sophisticated and the geometric folds speak volumes to his clientele, much in the same way that masons translated the language of symbols to their patrons.

status for the initiated, but no longer just the purview of very wealthy women. The vintage couture and designer markets have made these fabulous garments of yesteryear available to a wider clientele. But considerable intellect, strategy and effort must still be invested in order to acquire these garments and perhaps that accounts for the patina of class and wealth accorded the wearer.

There was a time when all most women could expect from their clothing was warmth and modesty. Only the tiniest minority could enjoy the stylish if not downright decadent clothing we associate with bygone eras. No more. Good clothes are everywhere. The very best, haute couture itself, can still be enjoyed by those willing to seek it out. Fine fashion is well within the reach of all women.

This mid-60s long, lean silhouette has a streamlined non-geometric feminine line. The classic design could be worn in any time period and be perfect. Originally designed in red crêpe by Valentino for Princess Luciana Pignatellias, it appeared in the May 1966 issue of *Life* magazine.

This suit is a Balenciaga creation. Balenciaga was arguably the greatest master and craftsman fashion has produced. The kingdom of Cristobal Balenciaga had dwindled by the late 1960s. Rather than becoming passé or unappreciated, Balenciaga retired and closed his fashion house in 1968. No one working for him was told of the closure; they found out via the press. Balenciaga died in 1972. Almost forty years later, we now have a better understanding of Balenciaga's genius for streamlined concepts of pure form.

What to know before you go

02

What to know before you go

I like my money right where I can see it — hanging in my closet.
Candace Bushnell (HBO series Sex and the City)

You've made a decision to boost your wardrobe IQ by seeking out some of the most coveted clothing in the fashion world. Perhaps you already own a piece or two. It is wise to learn as much as you can about the designer or couturier who created your garment.

Getting started: do your homework

You have made an investment in your wardrobe so investigate the name as you would any investment. Sitting on the sidelines of couture collection shows may still be an elite experience, but the virtual world provides instant gratification as images from the runways of Paris, Milan, New York and Tokyo are streamed and tweeted in real time. Prior seasons are archived online as well, allowing for an in-depth view of the designer's evolution, not to mention a "study guide" for recognizing past works when shopping in vintage or consignment stores to add to your investments. Visit these websites to witness the designer couture and ready-to-wear collections from anywhere on the globe:

- First View (www.firstview.com)
- Style (www.style.com)

Underdress from
Dior Suit on
page 29.

- Vogue (www.vogue.com)
- New York Magazine (www.nymag.com)

Libraries, bookstores and online retailers carry designer monographs and biographies. There are also fashion dictionary compilations, museum exhibition publications and documentaries providing interesting background history on these talented artists. Often they are as controversial and fascinating as their fashions. Searching online for designer interviews provides an insight into their personality and creative focus. An interview with the young Yves Saint Laurent or the most recent sound bite from Marc Jacobs is just a click away. In addition to knowing a couturier's personal history, it is important to understand a bit about the key components of the garment's construction that contribute to the quality and cost of couture clothing.

If you sell it, they will come

There are many different types of retail establishments selling luxury and designer discounted merchandise. Having an understanding of the different types of stores is critical, so that a true bargain can be recognized and appreciated. Here is a shortlist of the most visible establishments specializing in and offering discounted luxury goods.

Designer Resale Stores

These shops offer a variety of gently worn high-end designer clothing and accessories for sale. Items are a fraction of the original cost, and garments are cleaned and assessed before being placed on the sale floor. Most of these shops are independently owned and take items on consignment, so pricing is flexible. Styles are frequently from a past season; many shops list the season next to the price and the more current styles are priced accordingly.

Designer Outlet Stores

These larger establishments receive goods from manufacturers and can be directly related to the manufacturer. Although the merchandise is new, some defects may exist, and it is referred to as "off-price" goods. These items can be returns, over-cuts, or very slightly damaged.

Irregular Designer Merchandise Stores

Similar to designer outlet stores except they specialize in slightly damaged or returned merchandise. The items frequently have defects that are not prominently visible or problematic for the average consumer (example: size mismarks, button irregularities, etc).

Vintage Shops

Vintage merchandise is technically defined as anything over 25 years old. However, in relation to clothing and accessories, the term has become a catchall phrase for anything old. Vintage shops are where you will find the most unusual treasures to complement those great designer pieces and gain a distinct style. They are widely diverse and usually privately owned. Vintage shopping constitutes a real treasure hunt. The city guide in chapter 7 offers more extensive information about shopping vintage.

Charity and Secondhand Stores

Offering a wide variety of used clothing and accessories, these stores are frequently associated with a particular charity or cause. Tax-deductible donations are accepted and resold to the public. The purchase of these items at establishments in the US with official charitable status constitutes a tax-deductible donation, although this may not be the case in other countries. Check with an accountant or a tax website to find out, as the tax code frequently changes. Some of the best bargains are found in more affluent neighborhoods, as more upscale merchandise is being donated.

Tag, Garage, Lawn, or Moving Sales

These are not actual retail establishments, but private sales offered by individuals for a limited time frame. A trend is emerging in many countries to professionalize these modest events. Frequently with this new breed of garage sale, local advertising and sometimes payment options other than cash may be possible. The merchandise is still used and is being discarded, so look things over carefully before buying as there is usually no recourse to return faulty or damaged items.

Estate Sales

A more professional, upscale form of the traditional garage or tag sale. The person or company conducting the sale has the merchandise evaluated and priced, and a commission is paid. Sometimes these sales are conducted over several days and bids can be placed for more coveted items.

Fabric

The foundation of designer clothing is based on the quality of the material supporting its structure, drape and shape. Natural fibers (wool, silk, cotton, linen) are used generously, but it may be difficult to find fabric labels in many vintage garments. The United States passed the Wool Products Labeling Act in 1939, but not until the Textile Fiber Products Identification Act was approved in late 1958 did the widespread use of fabric labels become standard. The European Union has similar laws requiring the labeling of fiber content on clothing. Almost everything you will find from the first half of the 20th century will be made with natural fibers. This would also be true of any garment linings. Sometimes just "feeling" the material will give you a clue. The textile industry refers to this as "the hand of the fabric," otherwise known as assessing the quality of the fabric by how it feels to the touch. Cotton may feel cool, wool may feel scratchy and silk may feel dry or sticky.

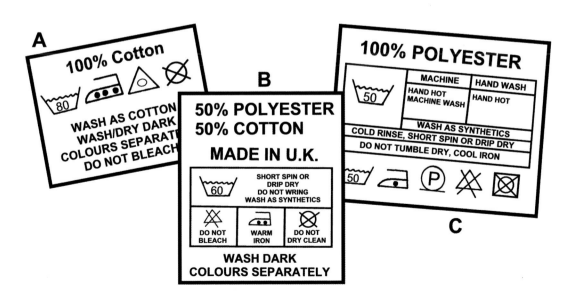

Synthetic fabrics were not used in couture clothing, for the most part, until the 1960s. If a Claire McCardell jumper or a Dior cocktail dress joins your closet inventory, you may have to rely on your sense of touch as well as sight to identify the material content, but it is a safe bet that the fabric will be natural. If it is wool, be sure to check for damage from moth holes. Back collar and neckline edges, under-arm seams and cuffs may have slight fiber breakdown due to perspiration or abrasion. Synthetic fabrics, developed to confound these drawbacks, may not show evidence of this type of damage, but may contain pulled threads or other signs of wear.

Sketch of a Jacques Fath evening gown by Rene Gruau.

(Right) The exquisite construction of a Jean Paul Gaultier jacket.

Construction

You can't judge a book by its cover, nor can you judge garment quality solely by evaluating the exterior. It is what's on the inside (or is unseen) that counts. Andre Leon Talley, contributing editor of *Vogue*, once stated that when a couture gown passes by him on the runway, he is imagining how exquisite it would look on the inside as well. The construction, or *guts*, of a garment is so important that museum exhibitions today include transparent and hollow dress forms allowing the viewer to see *inside* the garment.

Turning your garment inside out will truly expose the value of your piece. Noted American designer James

Galanos' use of quality fabrics and thoughtful garment cuts and construction have made him a living link between the French couture tradition and American ready-to-wear. Today's Ralph Rucci is the first American designer since Mainbocher to design ready-to-wear as well as being invited to show as an individual designer on the haute couture schedule.

 CHECKLIST: **CONSTRUCTION DETAIL**

- Turn the garment inside out.
- Look for obvious indications of alterations such as uneven stitching or a repair.
- Inspect the hem to see how much fabric is in the seam allowance. Facing may be used to keep the hem stiff and hanging away from the body. Chanel suits traditionally have a gold metal chain weight at the jacket hem to ensure that the garment hangs smoothly. Some dresses or skirts may also have weighted hems.
- Examine seams and darts. In couture construction, these are stitched down for additional stability as well as to eliminate bulk and maintain a smooth line in the outer garment. Couture garments have more darts and seams in places like the underarm, bust and waist to add more ease and a custom fit. The seam allowance edge is often finished with seam binding for a neat appearance and to prevent fabric from raveling.
- Study the additional layers of construction. A suit jacket or dress might have interfacing in the front to stabilize the shape, and in older garments flannel patches were often added for warmth. A cocktail dress may have a boned bodice, or corset-like infrastructure, to provide a foundation for strapless gowns or tops. All of these details will feature small, hand stitches.

- Consider the closures and fasteners: Observe tiny details such as small covered snaps and hook and eye fasteners. Hooks and eyes are used in waistbands, necklines and garment openings as additional insurance for a smooth fit. Covered snaps are often used to make lingerie strap guards, which prevent the bra strap from slipping. Buttonholes will be hand stitched or bound with fabric. Buttons will be covered with fabric or made of natural materials. Zippers have been used in couture since the early 1900s, but nylon zippers weren't introduced until the 1960s. A nylon zipper in a vintage couture garment will be an indicator of some alteration or repair.

As you inspect your garment inside out, you will notice the sheer perfection, thought and effort paid to the inside, which only the wearer will see. If it's not perfect inside, the garment isn't couture or it has been altered or repaired. Seam finishes and seam allowances are primary qualifiers for quality level. Hem allowances are generous, often at least two inches or more. Seam allowances should be at least one inch. The back hem in couture clothing may be a half-inch longer to balance the overall silhouette and flatter the derriere. The hemline itself may have garment weights inserted to ensure it falls well over the hips and will not pull or rise up. All seams are finished in couture, often by hand. Lapels, collars, cuffs and some waistbands will be interfaced, which helps support the shape. You can usually tell if something has interfacing, as it will feel more solid and structured, not limp or flimsy. Buttonholes are another sign of a couture garment. They are bound and usually hand finished. Buttons will be made from natural materials like leather or abalone, even glass, but not plastic. Often you'll see custom covered buttons in the same fabric as the garment.

What *affordable* means and how to determine your budget

If you ask your friends how much they spend on clothing, it's likely they won't know or say they spend too much. But to determine what affordable means to you, a budget of sorts is in order. Add up what you paid for all the clothing in your closet that you're NOT wearing. If you are like most of us, it is highly likely that you would have some money to work with just by changing your shopping habits.

Imagine that, instead of shopping impulsively or buying sale items that never make it out of the closet, you only replace or update basics and invest in one or two important pieces a year. Affordable doesn't necessarily mean cheap, but can be synonymous with thoughtful spending.

What kind of shopper are you?

Trend Scout

The Trend Scout looks for the season's must-haves and hot runway trends. She may not pay top dollar for name brands, opting for stylish interpretations of the current looks, but she's buying new things every season. Clothing that is too trendy can look dated quickly.

Sale Shopper

The Sale Shopper pays more attention to store sales versus the most current styles. She can justify the purchase because it seems like a bargain. These kinds of acquisitions often lead to orphans: a top with no matching skirt or pant, or vice versa.

Impulse Purchaser

The Impulse Purchaser is a social shopper. As she roams in and out of stores, something catches her eye: a spectacular shoe, a too-trendy belt, a cocktail dress on sale but a size too small. Frequently these things are worn once or not at all.

Need-it-Now Consumer

The Need-it-Now Consumer waits until the last minute to buy important pieces like a cocktail dress for a special occasion. In many cases she won't find what she's looking for, so subsequently she settles for something that isn't quite right due to time constraints. This pattern practically ensures the piece will be banished to the back of the closet, often never to be worn again.

Basics Buyer

The Basics Buyer only shops a few times a year for wardrobe staples like T-shirts, and replaces items like a business suit or winter coat when showing some signs of wear. Not a bad strategy, but this shopper rarely plans for the rest of her apparel needs, and often becomes a Need-it-Now Consumer as a result.

 CHECKLIST: **WORKING ON YOUR BUDGET**

- Take an inventory of clothing you bought in the past 12 months. Make a list by category: accessories; shoes; handbags; basics, T- shirts, intimate apparel, sportswear and active wear; cocktail or evening attire; and work clothes.
- Estimate approximately what each item cost and mark the amounts down.
- Based on this list, check off items you wear all the time and note the things you don't wear often or at all.
- Tally up category totals to find out what you spent.
- Add up the amounts for things you wear and the things you aren't wearing. These three numbers will give you some insight into your shopping habits and define your budget.

The practical fashion formula: CPW (cost per wear)

Just like any investment, you can look at variables. CPW is the cost per wear. For example, if you buy a Jean Paul Gaultier jacket from the 1990s for $1500/£815/€1180, and you wear it twice a week, in one year it will have cost $14.42/£7.84/€11.35 per wear. If you buy a colorful Oscar de la Renta maxi dress from the 1960s for $725/£393/€570 and only wear it three times in one year, then you're looking at about $218/£131/€190 per wear. But if that same dress is kept for three years, and worn nine times, then the cost per wear is about $81/£44/€64. Considering that some clothing could already be 30 or more years old, and taking the original cost into account, you've got a healthy handicap on the odds of finding something that's perfect for you and your lifestyle at an affordable price.

 TIP

Save your sales receipts for clothing purchases and tally up total expenditures at the end of the year. It can be a real eye-opener to discover how much you actually spend. Regardless of the amount, you might be pleasantly surprised to see what your true wardrobe budget is.

But is it real?

Handbags and leather goods are the gateway items for designer apparel. Carrying an expensive bag signals the desire to embody style. Owning a Louis Vuitton bag is *costume de rigueur* in certain circles. Other bags, like the Hermès Birkin, are almost mythic. The Birkin, named after actress/singer Jane Birkin (with an average price of $9000/£4900/€7085), is in such demand that, at one time there was a waiting list of up to two years to possess one. When you buy couture and designer goods at their own showroom stores or at in-store boutiques of reputable retailers, you are guaranteed the item is the real deal, for the real price. A Hermès coin purse can set you back almost $500. But who wants to pay retail? It's important, however, not to be duped into a *real steal*.

The counterfeit luxury apparel business is booming. Rick Ishitani, a Los Angeles police officer in charge of an elite squad specializing in the piracy of intellectual property and high-end apparel, states, "The estimated losses cost the world economy 500 billion dollars (326 billion pounds/ 392 billion euros) a year. Consumer appetite for luxury goods is huge. Everybody rich or poor likes a bargain. But the profits fund lavish lifestyles for the members of these organized crime syndicates and possible terrorist activities."

Don't buy anything on the street, end of story. Every major city has a neighborhood where purses, sunglasses, shoes and other stylish goods can be picked up inexpensively. In Los Angeles it's Santee Alley. In New York City it's Canal Street. In London it's around Oxford Street and the market stalls. Interestingly, in Paris you can be fined for carrying a fake bag and the item will be confiscated. Nobody selling stuff out of the trunk of their car has the goods either. If it's too good to be true, it's probably a fake.

Retailers specializing in gently worn designer handbags are flourishing online, including Bag Borrow or Steal (www.bagborroworsteal.com) offering weekly rentals of coveted bags from Vuitton, Prada, Chanel and Yves Saint Laurent. Marcy Carmack, co-founder of the resale website The Real Real (www.therealreal.com), says they have relationships with different designer houses and can send things in for them to authenticate. Several of the top online sellers of designer handbags, in fact, have what's called an authenticator on staff.

Luxury Exchange (www.luxuryexchange.com), the world's largest brokerage for luxury accessories, has an A rating from the Better Business Bureau in the United States. They work with the senior authenticator from My Poupette (www.mypoupette.com), an authority on trademarked designer merchandise and one of the first companies to offer authentication services. Angie Houston founded My Poupette in 1999 when she started seeing fake bags on eBay. Her burgeoning collection of over 300 Louis Vuitton pieces, all purchased new, was her inspiration to help people identify and purchase authentic luxury goods. My Poupette works with authenticators all over the world. According to Houston, "Approximately 80 percent of the bags we see are not the real thing, which makes a statement about how easy it is to be fooled."

✓ CHECKLIST: **HOW TO AVOID FRAUDULENT ONLINE PURCHASES**

- Look for the online seller's posted information about where they get their merchandise, as well as read their return and authentication policies. The language of the return policy is important. Some sellers "guarantee satisfaction," rather than guaranteeing authenticity, and they might charge a restocking fee.
- Think about the price of the item. There is reason to be cautious if an item regularly retails for hundreds or thousands of dollars and a site is selling it for a fraction of that cost, or describes it as a factory second or return.
- Pay for purchases with a credit card or PayPal so there is recourse in case the item is not authentic.
- Have the item authenticated quickly so that it can be returned if it turns out to be phony.

It's all in the details: you can spot a fake

Even if you can't get to a designer boutique or department store to look at the real thing, it's essential to do some advance research before you buy. Read fashion magazines, especially the spring and fall issues, when these publications are brimming with extravagant ads and fashion layouts for every designer imaginable. Go on the official websites of Louis Vuitton and other makers of luxury goods to get familiar with the hallmarks of their products. Most luxury goods companies will send out a catalogue if requested; studying photographs of the genuine items will empower you to spot fakes. Counterfeit goods keep getting better, making it harder to distinguish a replica, but there is always a flaw somewhere on a fake.

The Purse Blog (www.purseblog.com) is devoted to daily editorial, full of lush images, on all the hottest designer handbags. They have a forum focused on shopping resources, with thousands of linked threads, many devoted to the topic of counterfeits and authenticity. Luxe Designer Handbags (www.luxedesignerhandbags.com) has a series of videos on how to determine a bag's authenticity. Do your homework and you will be more capable of identifying the exquisite workmanship and characteristics that makes a brand's leather goods and accessories unique.

Counterfeit goods keep getting better, making it harder to distinguish a replica, but there is always a flaw somewhere on a fake.

Fake Vuitton with wrinkles and visible creases.

Poorly constructed fake Vuitton.

Machine stitched fake Vuitton

CHECKLIST: **SIX QUICK STEPS TO SPOT THE FAKE**

- Feel the bag. Real leather is supple and smooth, not stiff. Good leather doesn't feel cheap. Louis Vuitton is one of the most copied accessory lines. Their bags are made with a thick canvas that is perfectly pressed and has no wrinkles or visible creases. Fakes are packed tightly for shipping, so wrinkles are a dead giveaway.
- Study the construction. On a Louis Vuitton, the repeat pattern of the initials, L.V., will always line up on all sides, and never be cut off from view in a seam line. This is true of most designer bags with a pattern. Vuitton also uses a very light leather for buckles, handles and straps that darkens over time. Their handles also have a unique, but subtle, red dye on the edges of the leather. If you see any over-dye, loose threads or excess glue, it's not bona fide.
- Inspect the hardware. The heavy metal and artillery on real designer bags looks sturdy and feels heavy. It's never plastic. Zippers, grommets, studs and fasteners are stamped or engraved with the logo. Counterfeiters frequently stamp the hardware, so look at the quality of the metal and the stamp. The stamp will be evenly placed and legible. The metal will not be rough or have jagged edges.
- Examine the stitching. Since most designer bags are hand stitched, the stitching will be tight, consistent and slanted just slightly. Forgeries are machine stitched, which isn't slanted.
- Look inside the bag for identification tags. Louis Vuitton, Prada and Marc Jacobs are brands whose bags feature a tag with secret codes or serial numbers.
- Scrutinize the logo. Logos are distinctive and each brand has traits the fakes often don't bother to imitate. Prada bags have a metal plate that is always the same color as the bag. The leg of the R in their logo has a slight curve. Louis Vuitton uses a unique font.

Get ready to receive

Finding the best deals means having access to insider information. Create a special email address to use exclusively for the pursuit of couture. To make it easier to keep track of the various emails you are about to receive, set up some preferences in your email reader. Apple®'s Mac Mail and Microsoft® Office's Outlook let you set up folders. In Google Mail, you can create labels. It is wise to make a label or folder called Sample Sales, or Harrods or Vintage. This way you can sort, organize and classify these electronic notifications. You don't want to miss out on a good sale because an email ended up in your junk mail folder, so be sure to add the vendor address to your address book. Groundbreaking online boutiques offering exclusive designer merchandise at large price reductions include:

- *OutNet* (www.theoutnet.com)
- *Yoox* (www.yoox.com)
- *Gilt* (www.gilt.com)
- *HauteLook* (www.hautelook.com)
- *Cocosa* (www.cocosa.com)

Here you need not even leave your house to shop in stylish virtual boutiques. These resources have become so popular that designers now launch styles or ship exclusive pieces to these sites before they hit the brick and mortar stores.

Get in with the in crowd

Now the hunt begins. Getting on the best lists to receive advance notifications is key to finding exactly what you want. Systematically begin signing up to receive notifications from retailers and discounters that carry couture and your favorite designer labels. Register for free subscriptions and memberships to online flash and private sale sites as well as daily newsletters with the insider scoop.

A QUICK GUIDE TO JARGON

- A *pop-up* is a sale or event at a temporary location.
- A *flash sale* is the online version of a pop-up.
  Flash sales and pop-ups are available for a limited
  time. Some last only 24 hours, others up to four days.
- *Private sales* are for members only.
- *Affiliate programs* offer commissions to entrepreneurs and
  companies who drive traffic to a specific landing page within a
  website. Affiliate programs aren't all the same. The criteria to
  be eligible for participation and payment agreements are
  different from one program to another.
- *Shopper's Clubs* are often invitation-only and offer a limited
  amount of "curated" and "specially priced" products from
  luxury brands, for brief windows of time. This continues to
  create the sense of urgency and must-have fever often attached
  to luxury goods, without undermining the value of the brand.

Daily newsletters are the rage in the United States. These newsletters offer a carefully curated choice of newly discovered or sought-after products and services, as well as invites and deals. Daily Candy (www.dailycandy.com) writes up one cool thing a day, and regularly includes roundups of sample sales. Daily Candy has 12 city centric editions – 11 cities in the United States and one for London. In 2011, they rolled out a geo-location content delivery app, Daily Candy Stylish Alerts. The application delivers the company's signature fashion content to users in proximity of current local happenings like designer sales.

Vente-Privee (www.vente-privee.com), the godmother of online flash sales, has been around for over 20 years. With sites for France,

Germany, Spain, Italy, the UK, Belgium, Austria and the Netherlands, Vente-Privee's discounts are 50 to 70 percent off designer brands. The Secret Sample Sale (www.secretsamplesale.co.uk) in London works with such designers as Vivienne Westwood, Dolce & Gabbana, Gucci and Prada to unload excess stock and samples, offering special, members-only shopping days, with up to 90 percent off the original retail price. Designer Sales UK (www.designersales.co.uk) provides members with insider news updates, invites and member discounts for designers including Cavalli, Valentino, Chloé and Versace.

The Fashion Lisst – and yes it's spelled Lisst – in the Netherlands (www.thefashionlisst.com) claims to offer Europe's largest designer stock and sample sales. Discounted designer goods range from Gucci and Alexander McQueen to Balenciaga, Dior, Sonia Rykiel and Marc by Marc Jacobs. These are just a few examples of where you can save money on designer garments.

 TIP

To find more websites that will alert you to money saving deals Search the Internet using keywords like:

> Sample sale
> Flash sale
> Private sale
> Shopper's club
> Member's only sale
> Designer sale

 CHECKLIST FOR SUCCESS: **YOU CAN ALWAYS GET WHAT YOU WANT, WHETHER ON FOOT OR ON THE KEYBOARD**

- Arrive early, before the store opens, to get access to the best selection.
- Pay attention to email alerts; open them immediately to ensure you don't miss important sale dates or special offers.
- Use a calendar. Note dates of upcoming sales and events on a calendar. If you use a cloud-based calendar, like Google Calendar or iCal, you can create reminders and alarms that generate an email or pop-up on your smart phone or computer screen.
- Use social media to your advantage. Look for the Twitter site or the Facebook page of stores and sites you shop. Follow them on Twitter as well. Often retailers use social media to offer promo codes for free shipping, exclusive offers and discounts.
- Become friendly with the sales associates at your favorite discount and designer resale stores. Let them know what you're looking for in both brands and price. Ask if they work on commission. If so, they're more likely to notify you when things go on sale.
- Work with personal shoppers. Many stores call this service "shop by appointment." The personal shopper services are usually free. It's like having your own personal stylist. These personal shoppers will notify you in advance of exclusive sales and events.
- Use store charge cards when possible. Cardholders benefit from perks programs with a range of bonuses such as complimentary cuff and hem alterations, extra discounts, early notification of sales or rewards points. Some retailers extend a one time, special discount on your first purchase when you apply for their store card. If you sign up for a store card to buy merchandise that's marked down, the additional discount could add up to sizable savings. The trick is to pay the balance off each month; otherwise you're going to lose any savings to the high interest rates these types of cards charge.
- Learn about affiliate programs. Some online retailers pay a commission for sales generated via links on fashion forward websites and blogs. If you blog or own a fashionable website, you might qualify for participation.

Identify authentic designer goods by their label. Here are some examples of more popular designer labels. Authentic designer goods will always have woven labels and not printed labels.

It should be noted that the older couture pieces will frequently not have labels as it was a common practice to cut them out in order to avoid international taxes and import tariffs.

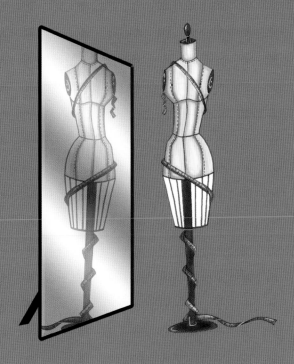

But will it fit?

03

But will it fit?

"Fashion is architecture... it is a matter of proportions."
Coco Chanel

Unless you are collecting couture and designer items to be archived and do not plan to wear them, then you need to think about fit. Couture and designer clothing is expensive, luxurious, and often unique. The principles of actually wearing couture clothing are easily understood if you strategically approach the end result – to look great in the clothing you've purchased. Just because the garment itself is utterly amazing does *not* mean you'll look utterly amazing in it. You have a lifestyle. Your clothes have a lifestyle. They go wherever you go, allow you to do whatever you do, *if* they fit.

What size is it? What size am I?

These are really good questions and may not have a standard answer. Regardless of what size the label reads – if there even is a size label – a secondhand garment, for example, may have been altered. Women's clothing size specifications have changed over the years. Today's contemporary sizes 4-6 (USA sizing) would be a size 12 in garments produced in the 1950s. The rumors that Marilyn Monroe wore a size 16 at some point in her life could be true, based on the

evolution of women's apparel sizing. Research and gossip suggest that in 1956, the 5'5" (165 cm) Monroe's actual measurements were a 37-inch (94-cm) chest, a 24-inch (61-cm) waist, and 37-inch (94-cm) hips. Over sixty years later, using The Gap's 2011 sizing chart, Marilyn's chest adds up to a US size 10, with her waist measurement a size 1 or XS (Extra Small). However, today's US size 16 measures out as a 42-inch (107-cm) chest, a 32.5-inch (82.5-cm) waist and a 41.5-inch (105.4-cm) hip.

There are really no standard specifications for women's clothing sizes. Every manufacturer determines the sizing of the garments they produce, creating confusion among shoppers who are asking, "What size am I?" Remember Millicent Robert's Barbie doll? American toy manufacturer Mattel created "Barbie" in 1959. If she were an actual girl, Barbie would stand 5'9" (175 cm), with a 39-inch (99-cm) chest, an 18-inch (46-cm) waist, and a 33-inch (84-cm) hip measurement. In the late 1990s she was redesigned with a wider waist to accommodate current fashions of the times, but even she would have issues in ready-to-wear, asking "What size am I?" as well.

Vanity [sizing], thy name is woman

Even though Shakespeare's Hamlet did not utter the often-misquoted phrase, "Vanity, thy name is woman," vanity sizing does exist! Every designer has a muse or "fit model" they reference when designing and fitting. If that fit model has, for instance, a longer arm length, chances are that the designer brand's sizing will have a more generous sleeve length. This, too, can wreak havoc with assuming a standard size will be a standard size across the board. Dave Bruner, Technology Development Vice-President at TC2, a company known for their technological innovations for the apparel industry, claims the original standard sizing specifications in the United States originated from 1940s-950s statistical data. "Widespread use of what's called *vanity sizing* is a marketing tool," said Bruner, "since someone is more likely to buy a garment marked as a smaller size."

International size variations

Europe uses different sizing scales and numbering. A size *medium* in the US could be a Size 38 or 40 in the United Kingdom, or a 42 or 44 in Italy. These numbers don't seem to correlate to anything specific; rather, they appear to be arbitrary, adding to the befuddlement of what size you need.

CLOTHING SIZE CHART						
COUNTRY	AUSTRALIA	US	UK	ITALY	JAPAN	FRANCE
XXS	6	0 - 2	6	38	5	34
XS	8	2 - 4	8	40	7	36
S	10	4 - 6	10	42	9	38
M	12	6 - 8	12	44	11	40
L	14	8 - 10	14	46	13	42
XL	16	10 - 12	16	48	15	44

SHOE SIZE CHART					
AUSTRALIA	ITALY	US	UK	JAPAN	FRANCE
5	36	6	3	22	37
5.5	36.5	6.5	3.5	22.5	37.5
6	37	7	4	23	38
6.5	37.5	7.5	4.5	23.5	38.5
7	38	8	5	24	39
7.5	38.5	8.5	5.5	24.5	39.5
8	39	9	6	25	40
8.5	39.5	9.5	6.5	25.5	40.5
9	40	10	7	26	41
9.5	40.5	10.5	7.5	26.5	41.5

IMPERIAL & METRIC CONVERSIONS											
INCHES	26	27	28	29	30	31	32	33	34	35	36
CENTIMETERS	66	69	71	74	76	79	81	84	86	89	91

Continuing to confuse everyone is the fairly recent (2006) introduction of the European Size Designation of Clothes, referred to as EN13402, based on the metric system and 1990s anthropometric studies. Translation: Consumer bodies have changed, anthropologically speaking, over the decades. This sizing standard is intended to replace older sizing systems, but as yet hasn't been widely accepted. Since most of the vintage clothing you find is much older, the updated 1990s information won't be of much help.

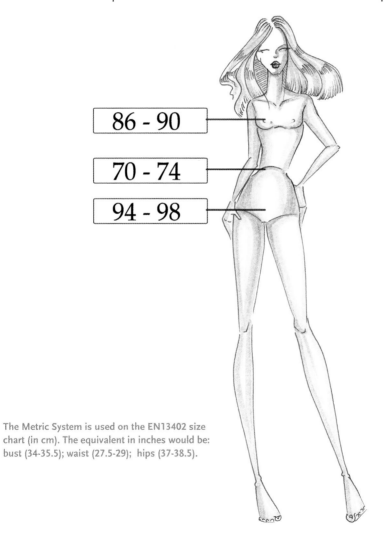

86 - 90

70 - 74

94 - 98

The Metric System is used on the EN13402 size chart (in cm). The equivalent in inches would be: bust (34-35.5); waist (27.5-29); hips (37-38.5).

If you S-T-R-E-T-C-H it, it will fit

Twentieth-century innovations in apparel, including performance fabrics, microfibers and the advent of Lycra® spandex and other stretch fibers available in ready-to-wear have spoiled us with easy-to-wear and easy-to-care-for clothing. This wasn't always the case.

Joyce Michel, the founder of GoBe, a company that makes performance apparel for active people with the tag line, "Life without Friction," was one of the first six design assistants hired by Donna Karan for Donna Karan New York; Karan tasked Michel with the directive to "bring her something new." Michel quickly suggested that she add stretch to her woven garments. Lycra® had been around since the 1960s, but until then had only been used in knits. Donna Karan bought luxury fabrics from the top textile companies in Italy, who also sold to the couture houses. According to Michel, Donna Karan was the first designer to use Lycra® in woven fabrics, and as a result the Italian textile firms began to offer stretch fabrics to the couturiers, which led to the inclusion of stretch in couture collections, and created the demand for the use of stretch fibers in almost every apparel category today.

Famed retailer Rita Watnick, has amassed the largest collection of haute couture in the world at her emporium Lily et Cie in Beverly Hills, California. According to Watnick, "The intent for couturiers who use fabrics with stretch is not to accommodate size or comfort; it's because clothing with stretch fibers wears better, wrinkles less and designers can make things really tight."

The Italian textile firms began to offer stretch fabrics to the couturiers

It's only a number – how to measure your body

Remember, haute couture is made for one specific person's measurements, and prêt-à-porter or ready-to-wear is made to a size. Almost everyone can point to a number of different sized garments hanging in their closets, as we've determined clothing sizes do vary by designer. Knowing your measurements is tantamount to making successful choices for your collection, especially if you are purchasing online. You might ask a friend to help you out with this measuring project, as you'll be taking more than just your bust, waist and hips. You'll need to have access to these numbers when you're shopping, so make sure to take good notes, or fill in the chart below and save the collected data. It is a good idea to remeasure yourself several times a year if your weight tends to yo-yo or you lose or gain more than 5 pounds.

MY MEASUREMENTS
Date:
Height_____
Weight_____
1. Bust (around front to back) _____
2. Waist (around front to back)_____
3. Hips (around front to back)_____
4. Tops of Thigh (around)_____
5. Inseam (length of inner leg)_____
6. Shoulders (around front to back)_____
7. Upper Arm (around)_____
8. Arm length (shoulder to elbow)_____
9. Lower Arm (elbow to wrist)_____

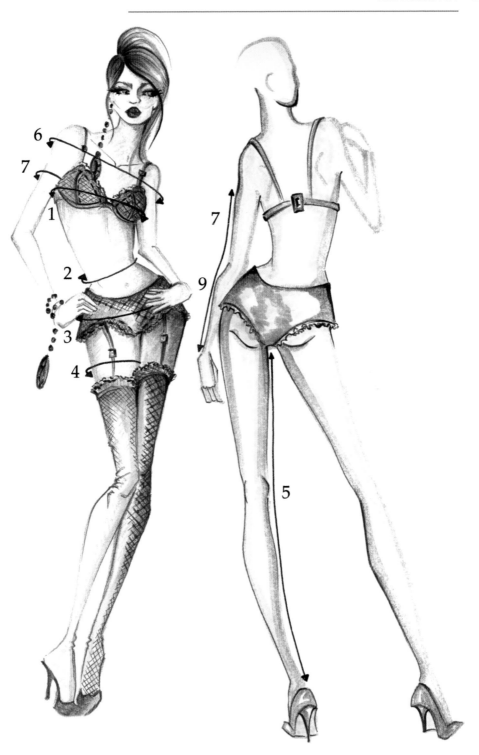

Knowing what works for you

Experts say it's a good idea to measure some of your own clothing as well. Understanding what works for you as well as why it works is the key to making wise purchases. Select different items from your wardrobe; focus on garments that fit well and look terrific on you. Then measure these stand-out garments. This will give you insight into how your measurements correlate to what works well on your body. It can help you to assess and determine some of your physical features, like broad shoulders, and body type (in terms of overall shape). Ask yourself some basic questions:

- Are you larger below the waist?
- Do you have an hourglass figure?
- Are your shoulders narrow or sloping?

Analyzing your measurements and studying yourself in the mirror will provide the knowledge and ergo the confidence necessary to make better investment purchases.

From Greek to sleek, how to figure it out

The ancient Greeks had a proportional standard of beauty that was a ratio of two to one, meaning the waist was half of the size of the shoulders and the hips and the shoulders were approximately the same – the original hourglass-shaped figure. Varieties of fruit and geometric shapes have been co-opted to describe women's body types, for example apple or pear, triangle or rectangle. These over-simplifications may help to streamline the process of figuring out how to look better in your clothes.

However, to simplify things even more, consider the relationship that your hips and shoulders have to your waist. Here are some of the basic shapes and guides for understanding those figure types.

Shoulders are wider than hips

Referred to as the "Apple," this figure type has shoulders that are often broad and straight, with a smallish bust, and thin legs. Your middle section may be slightly thick. Short skirts frequently work well to show off great legs. Choose clothing with a V-neck, keyhole or deep U-neck. Look for styles with raglan and dolman sleeves, and drop or set-in sleeves (inside the natural shoulder line). Vests and halter style tops look terrific with a wider shoulder. The best lapels are narrow, notched or vertical like a tuxedo; rolled and shawl collars are also advisable. Tunic tops, belted or not, surplice and blouson tops are also good choices. Trench coats, blazers, one-button, Ike and peplum-style jackets work best with wide shoulders. Just about any skirt style or shape works with this body type. Try to avoid square shape silhouettes, double-breasted jackets, shoulder pads, fussy or wide lapels, boat necklines, puffy sleeves and bulky sweaters.

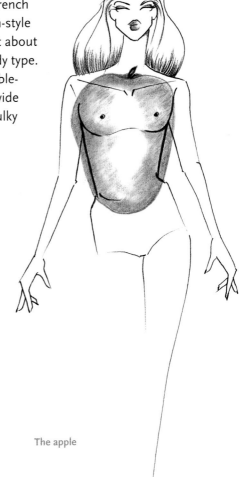

Short skirts frequently work well to show off great legs

The apple

Hips are wider than shoulders

This figure shape is referred to as the "Pear" and is usually larger below the waist, often with a smallish bust and narrow or sloping shoulders. The lower part of your torso may be larger in three different ways: either as a tummy bulge, a protruding derrière, or wider upper thighs. You want to draw attention away from the hip area. This could be accomplished with dramatic necklines and shoulder detailing created to balance out the figure and draw the eye up. Choose clothing that emphasizes the waist and skims the lower half of the body. A-line skirts and dresses are preferable. Collars can be wide and interesting. Balance out the body with these necklines: Grecian, square, scoop bateau, off the shoulder, sweetheart and décolleté. Look for shoulder details like pads or epaulettes, along with a variety of sleeve styles like capped, dolman, kimono, peasant and petal. Avoid blouson styles and banded hem tops.

The pear

Shoulders and hips are balanced

The
hourglass

Not all balanced figures are curvy. When there are more curves, this body is often referred to as an hourglass shape. Elizabeth Taylor and Marilyn Monroe epitomized curviness like this. Just about all the various styles of necklines, sleeves, skirts, dresses and jackets work in the case of the fairly balanced body. The key with an hourglass shape is to avoid clothes that add bulk or accentuate more roundness. For example, if the bust is fuller, avoid breast pockets, round collars, shawl or tuxedo style lapels, and anything with a wrap belt. Because your small waist is a strong asset, belted dresses and fitted waistline silhouettes are flattering for this figure type.

Hips and waist are the same

The rectangle

This figure shape is often described as a rectangle. However, your body can be straight or curvy, often with a smaller bust. Many styles are appropriate for this versatile figure type. To insinuate a waistline, look for blouses, jackets, dresses and coats with princess styling. Princess style incorporates vertical seams or darts in the front and back of a garment, gracefully insinuating a more balanced figure. Cowl and draped necklines can add length creating a central focal point. Geometric necklines open up the body and full, or gathered, skirts provide proportion. Silhouettes that flatter this figure type are blouson, chemise, dropped waist and empire style. Coatdresses, surplice-style dresses, tent dresses and unbelted shifts work well to balance out the torso. Wear layers, shirts with breast pockets or safari-style details to add shape and dimension. Choose belts that are the same color as the garment. The key is to de-emphasize the waist.

Fashion foundation

Regardless of what body type you think you are, fashion has a way of making us into the shape of the moment. If you look at photographs of fashionable clothing from the 1950s, you'll notice the bust shapes were more conical. This is the opposite of clothing from the 1920s and 1930s where the bust was not emphasized. Chanel had introduced sportswear and women were finally free of corsets. Today's popular bra styles are more rounded and often padded.

In order to ensure older clothing fits well, you may need to find bras that help shape your bust differently. A minimizer style bra might be helpful if you have a fuller bust, especially if the garment is

I dreamed I went to work in my maidenform* bra

One of the first ads Maidenform ever placed. Called "I Dreamed The Office," the ad showcases the Chansonette® bra, which featured signature circular stitching that uplifted the breasts to create the iconic cone-shaped look.

form-fitting. Minimizers redistribute the breast tissue so the bust doesn't stick out.

To get a better idea of the variety of bras available to the consumer today, investigate the online bra resources. Shipping is frequently inexpensive and widely available. Online shops such as Linda's (www.lindasonline.com) has retail stores in New York City, carries 200 bra sizes, and offers worldwide delivery. Knowing your shape and what flatters that shape will make your purchasing decisions more effective.

 TIPS FOR FIT AT BRICK & MORTAR

If you're hunting in a store and you find a coveted item, you can immediately determine whether you can wear it or not. Hold it up to your body in front of a mirror. Sometimes you can tell if it will fit just by looking at it, but to save time, and possible heartache in the dressing room, get out your tape measure. Try on the garment if possible. You'll need to take a few things into account. Hold the garment in your hands to analyze the drape, or ease, of the fabric. Pull on it, then let go to see if the fabric is stiff or diaphanous. Look at the details:

- Where are the seams?
- What is the shape or silhouette (empire, A-line, or column, for example) of the garment?
- What type of collar does it have?
- What is the orientation and color of any trim, buttons, zippers and pockets? (Details like these are great for what we refer to as optical illusion dressing.)

Human beings have grown taller and larger over the last century. Just look at the size of movie star imprints at the famed Chinese Theater in Hollywood, California. Some of the vintage clothing, couture, and resale designer clothing on the market today will be smaller due to the older comparative sizing guidelines. Current couture and designer clothing will be available in a wider variety of sizes. But knowing where you stand in terms of shape, dimensions and body proportions will help you make more flattering figure choices.

There is a long-standing tradition at the Chinese Theater in Hollywood for stars to press their hands and feet into cement squares in the courtyard.

Ten key pieces you
should own

04

Ten key pieces you should own

"You can have everything in life if you dress for it."
Edith Head

The workhorses of every wardrobe are classic pieces that never go out of style. In the history of couture, there are a few key designs that continue to stand the test of time. Although every season, the arbiters of fashion attempt to sift through the designers' offerings to generate what's referred to as the "must haves," there are some items which continue to make the list of garments one shouldn't be without year after year.

Investment dressing: quality, not quantity

Everything new on the runway has referenced the past, in some way, shape or form. Some styles recur on a fairly regular basis, for example hems may be mid-thigh one year, ankle-length the next, then back to mid-thigh the following year. Designers may also revisit their own backlist of designs and reissue a style from many seasons past. You can create your own reference wardrobe with styles that you will revisit again and again, by investing in quality pieces in styles that will never be "dated." While your personal style will inevitably evolve, the icons listed here will serve as a foundation for a wardrobe that is not only a good investment, but will also ensure that you are ready for any occasion.

Select the blazer that flatters your figure. Many blazer styles are available.

This shopping list really is the "bread and butter" of your wardrobe. These items are the basics you will always need and which you can embellish with accessories (jewelry, great shoes, sunglasses, hats, purses, etc.), adding or subtracting according to your taste or the occasion. Remember that, depending on your personality, you can opt to go for the extreme or the classic look – you decide. All ten pieces allow for versatility in function and style, and are figure-flattering no matter what your size. Don't forget the tips in chapter 3 about fit.

This Chanel black evening skirt worn with a basic black sweater is always classic and sophisticated.

The Icon list

1. The Blazer or Jacket

The fitted, boxy or double-breasted fully lined black blazer in wool crepe, linen or gabardine is the most versatile and constant item in your wardrobe. Consider investing in several versions. The price range for a good blazer or jacket can range from $130-180 (£70-98/€102-142) for designer resale and $150-275 (£80-149/ €118-216) for discounted new merchandise.

When shopping for a blazer, keep in mind that this will be an item that gets a lot of wear, so quality is key. Clean finished seams, high-end fabrics and flattering proportions are important features to consider in your selection. Designers Donna Karan, Giorgio Armani, Max Mara, Michael Kors, Ralph Lauren, Calvin Klein, Hugo Boss for women, all strive to create blazers that incorporate clean lines and classic tailoring.

 TIPS: WHAT TO LOOK FOR IN A BLAZER OR JACKET

- Lined blazers (the garment will hold up better).
- Buckram interlining (another mark of quality, helps the garment retain its shape).
- Back vent (an opening slit in the back allows for ease and better fit).
- Wider seam allowances (to allow for adjustments).
- Natural fabrics (silk, linen, wool, cashmere, camel hair or cotton).
- Buttons (quality buttons will be in precious and semi-precious materials: horn, abalone, jet, brass, mother of pearl).
- Buttonhole construction (tailored handcrafted buttonholes or quality machine buttonholes are a sign of distinction).
- Special finishing details (inside pocket, welted breast pocket, boutonniere).

Most designers offer well-crafted blouses or classic white shirts.

Consider a classic single-breasted blazer as your wardrobe staple such as this example from Donna Karan. The fabric and style details can vary from basic to extreme fashion silhouettes.

2. The White Blouse

Nothing frames the face better than the crisp silhouette of a white blouse. Look for a classic stand-up, portrait, ruffled or Peter Pan collar version in cotton, silk or linen. This versatile item can be worn with trousers by day or dressed up for evening with a great satin skirt, leggings or jeans – whatever your style. The key here is getting the right fit that doesn't gap over your bust or pull across the shoulders. The price range will vary from $50-100 (£28-54/€40-80) for designer resale and allow slightly more for discounted new pieces. Most designers offer well-crafted blouses or classic white shirts. Some names to look for are Carolina Herrera, Michael Kors, Oscar de la Renta, Valentino, Plein Sud, Akris, Pink or Kate Spade who all offer classic styling.

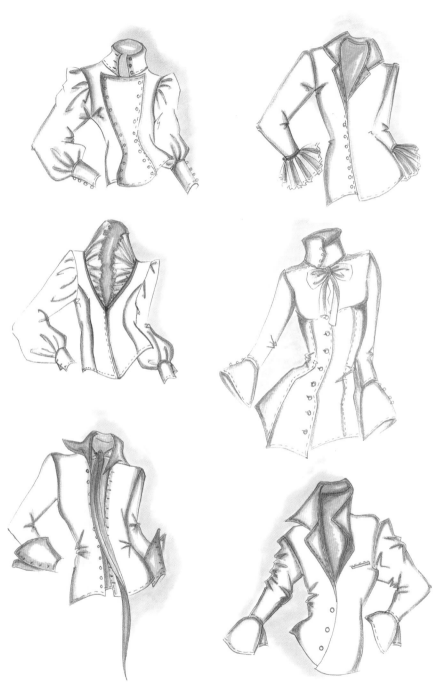

The white blouse can go day to evening and has unlimited potential.

3. The Chemise or Little Black Dress [LBD]

The Chemise, by definition, is simple and clean-lined. The wonderful thing is that it can be in almost any style, silhouette or fabric, and yet remain elegant. A useful price guide is to allow $125-200 (£70-125/€100-160) for designer resale and slightly higher for discounted new merchandise. Consider investing in several of these; the LBD never looks dated and it always remains chic. Every generation rediscovers this classic garment; it can be noted that America's First Lady, Michelle Obama choose a Michael Kors [LBD] for her first official White House portrait.

(Above) The LBD can be accessorized for day or evening looks. Consider it a blank canvas on which to impart your own personal style and flair.

(Right) The LBD shown here with gloves is a modern version of the *Breakfast At Tiffany's* dress designed by Givenchy in 1961.

The chemise has evolved and the little black dress isn't necessarily black – consider the more unique options available.

4. The Statement Coat

The concept of "coat" can be broadly defined. From the drama of a cape that can go from day to night, to the versatility of a swing coat, to the double-breasted reefer coat, to the classic trench coat, there is a multitude of style choices. In choosing the style or styles to invest in, consider how the coat will work with your other clothing: for example, a roomy coat or cape allows you to cover voluminous tops or dresses, while a more fitted coat will cut a lean silhouette over more slender garments. In terms of color, you can't go wrong if you choose a dark color or a classic camel or beige. Depending on the type of coat, fabrics to look for are cashmere, vicuña, velvet or fine wool or

heavyweight cotton for a trench coat. The prices will range from $75-250 (£40-150/€60-200) for a vintage find. Expect to pay around $200-350 (£110-190/€160-275) for higher quality designer resale or discounted new merchandise. Some vintage brands to look for are: Ann Klein, Lilli Ann, Valentino, Courrèges, Bonnie Cashin, Givenchy, YSL, Escada and, of course, Burberry for trench coats.

(Above) 1950s gold raw silk swing coat with exquisite tailoring, bought at a flea market for $24/£15/€18.

(Right) This fabulous Dior coat is a dramatic example of the statement coat.

More classic styling for
the statement coat.

5. The Basic Black Skirt

The black skirt, whether a figure-hugging pencil style, one that is gathered at the waist to fall smoothly over the hips, or an A-line style which gently flares from waist to hem... whatever the geometry, this must-have icon will work beautifully with the white blouse, the twinset, the blazer, coat or turtleneck. You should take into consideration the appropriate length for your figure when selecting a skirt and also whether it will be worn for casual wear or for business attire, for example. Look for skirts that have a lining as they will hang more smoothly. Fabrics such as fine wool, linen, silk or cotton are all appropriate. Depending on the fabric, you should expect to spend in the range of $75-150 (£40-85/€60-120) for designer resale or discounted new merchandise.

The basic skirt and white blouse are given a chic attitude simply by adding accessories.

6. The Trouser

The trouser, the pant, the slack... call it what you will, but this basic is a great way to dress up or dress casually in comfort. A well-made black or neutral pinstripe tailored pant in a quality fabric, properly fitted, will be a flexible wardrobe staple. As with the basic skirt above, trousers that are lined will hang better. Among the designers to look for are Helmut Lang, Stella McCartney, MaxMara, and Diane von Furstenberg. There are various styles to consider as well, for example the classic straight cut trousers or the wide leg versions. As before, consider what flatters your figure in deciding what to choose. For evening wear, silk palazzo-style trousers are also an elegant choice. Price Range: $50-125 (£30-70/€40-100) for designer resale or discounted new merchandise.

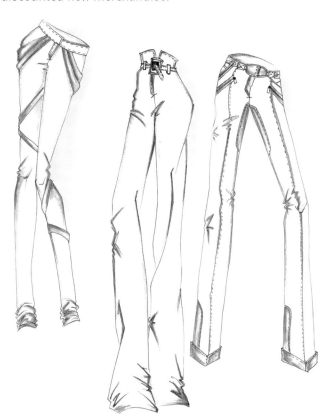

Consider alternative trouser styling.

7. The Evening Skirt – from Cocktail to Night

Who needs a "dressy dress" when many events are somewhere in-between. Pair a sleek black satin evening skirt – you guessed it – with that great white blouse or turtleneck or T-shirt. Crepe silk, silk satin or taffeta all create a dramatic silhouette. While one often thinks of evening skirts as being full length, in fact a shorter skirt in a dressy fabric can be right for all but the most formal occasions. The price range for an evening skirt can be from $50-125 (£30-70/€40-100) for vintage, designer resale or discounted new merchandise.

(Above) A fabulous black taffeta evening skirt can be very formal or simply chic after-five wear. Consider wearing with a T-shirt as Sharon Stone did at the Academy Awards this is considered "creative black tie."

(Right) A great evening skirt will work wonders for creative after-five look. Add accessories to personalize.

8. The Investment Legging

The 1980s basic black legging (aka ski pant) keeps returning, thus granting it *classic* status. With every new fabric technology, these spandex-blended wonders not only act as body-shapers, but also cut a clean line as a foundation for statement-making coats, blazers, mini dresses, etc. You can get leggings at a variety of price ranges, but the quality will be better if you spend a bit more. Also, keep in mind that heavier leggings are more forgiving and flattering. The price range for leggings is $25-75 (£15-40/€20-60) for discounted new merchandise.

The investment legging can be paired with a T-shirt and suit. This combination is a great way to change a suit look.

9. Twinset, Turtleneck and T-Shirt

These items are absolute basics for any wardrobe. The twinset can function as a polished jacket replacement and could even be worn with the evening skirt. The twinset combines a matching pullover and a cardigan. The pullover might be sleeveless, short-sleeved or occasionally long-sleeved. Choosing black or neutrals in cashmere or fine wool will provide you with the most versatility. The prices for designer resale and discounted new merchandise will range from $90-225 (£50-125/€70-180) and will also depend on whether the set is cashmere or wool.

Be it V-neck, U-neck, jewel or bateau, a basic silk or high quality cotton, the T-shirt is irreplaceable. Fit is important and if you are considering a classic white T-shirt then it must be kept pristine.

The classic turtleneck, be it mock or traditional, can be sleeveless, short-sleeved, three-quarter or long-sleeved. Look for these knits in quality cotton, silk, merino wool or cashmere. A well-made turtleneck should keep its shape and not stretch out at the neck. However, if you have a large bust this style may not be as flattering as it emphasizes the bust.

The price range for both T-shirts and turtlenecks can be anywhere from $10-80 (£7-45/€10- 65) in specialty stores or discounted new merchandise.

A Balenciaga suit. Consider the cost per wear formula, which will enable you to feel satisfied about your investment.

10. The Great "Art Piece" Designer Suit

You have heard of the *statement* necklace, the *statement* shoe and the *statement* coat. Well, this suit should be a conversation piece and make its own statement. This is probably the largest investment you will make in your wardrobe so choose the designer you love and admire. If you adore Dior, or crave Chanel, this is the time and place to make that investment, whether in vintage, resale or new. You should allow at least $400 (£220/€315) or more in your budget. How much more is at your discretion.

> *You can create your own reference wardrobe with styles that you will revisit again and again*

The suit you choose doesn't have to be a classic; this is a chance to reflect your own style.

 TIP: CONSIDER ALTERATION

Consider altering vintage finds – or any piece you desire. Don't pass on a unique item because of its length, shoulder pads or less-than-desirable buttons. All can be easily transformed.

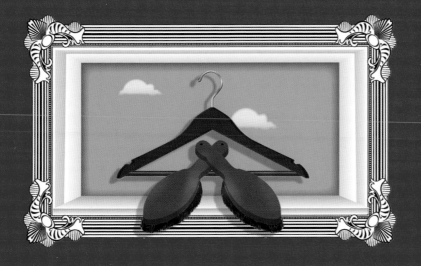

How to care for your couture wardrobe

05

How to care for your couture wardrobe

"Like buying a Ferrari or a race horse, you need to give your designer clothes a little extra attention and care."
John Anthony

Clothes need a place to live, breathe and thrive. People who like to shop and collect clothing require closet space and easy access to storage. Frequently, things you haven't worn in years are mixed in with the workhorses of your day-to-day wardrobe, taking up crucial space and making it time-consuming to get dressed.

Get ready to edit

Unless you are very lucky and have loads of closet space, most people find that closet space is at a premium. In addition, many closets are crammed full of clothing that isn't being worn. It is said most people only wear 20 percent of the clothing they own. Overcrowding is harmful for clothes, causing wrinkles, creases, potential snags and tears. If any of this sounds familiar, get ready to make some edits. Your investments will appreciate, literally and figuratively, when you evaluate and edit.

The closet is where the heart is

A closet audit simply means really taking a look at your closet both in terms of its contents as well as how it is organized. It's like an investigation. Your goals are to explore what is actually in your closet and to organize it in such a way that when it comes to wearing, caring for and storing your clothes, you're able to use every inch of available space. Auditing will help eliminate some of the 80% of unworn clothes undeserving of a home in your closet. Determine where and how you are going to keep your collectible couture, and where you will hang or fold your everyday wardrobe.

FINDING MORE CLOSET STORAGE

- Evaluate your current closet real estate. If you have more than one, can the contents of one closet be edited to hold more long-term storage? Consider reconfiguring any closet to access all usable space.
- Measure the height, width and depth of usable space in each closet. This information will be useful should you choose to purchase storage containers, add shelving, clothing bars and other closet organization components.
- Analyze your home for hidden storage. Review availability in all cupboards and drawers in every room of the house. That "junk" drawer could be emptied out and put to use storing sweaters, shoes or accessories. Is there room under your bed to store shoes or other things that don't require much height? If you have a staircase, consider the possibility of opening up the area underneath the stairs.
- Basements and attics are not the ideal location for storing couture clothing, unless you can ensure climate control and protection from pests and water damage that may be caused by a leaky roof or flood.

Closet audit checklist

As a first step, get everything out of the closet that doesn't work for you right now, including anything that needs cleaning or repair. You don't have to discard it all, just prioritize. It helps to know what's really *in* your closet to put together a game plan for editing your wardrobe and learning how to better organize it all. Your goal is to maintain a chic inventory. The phrase "quality, not quantity" can never be repeated enough. What's actually in your closet? A dress bought on sale but never worn, a pair of pants that never fit right, or a skirt with a ripped hem? Donate the dress and pants; drop the dress off at your tailor.

When space is at a premium, you have to be more discerning and move lower priority clothing to the back. If something goes into a bag or box, label and date the item. Why date it? Take an inventory once a year to tighten things up. If you see the item is something you haven't touched in a year, it's time to reevaluate it. If it's not a good interpretation of recurring trends, think about selling, donating or trading it to make room for garments you can wear now.

ANSWER THESE FEW QUESTIONS IN ORDER TO BEGIN THE PROCESS:

1. Do you have winter and summer clothes in the same closet? Could you store the off-season items elsewhere?
2. Are your work clothes hanging next to play clothes?
3. Are your shoes all over the place? Could they be organized in boxes or stored on the back of a door or under the bed?
4. Do you have some past "oldies but goodies" casting a sentimental shadow? If not worn regularly, they could be stored.
5. Ask yourself what can be removed and stored elsewhere?
6. What haven't you worn lately? Is it worth keeping?

7. Could you reconfigure your closet by adding a hanging bar; perhaps one for dresses, slacks and coats, and two for shorter items like tops, skirts and jackets? Is there room to add a shelf?

8. Measure your closet – height, width and depth. Knowing the exact amount of space you have to work with will save you time when you're looking for organizers. Look for under-utilized space as an inspiration for your closet makeover. Every "running foot" of rod should hold six items.

A well-organized closet.

 TIP: ORGANIZING YOUR CLOSET

Store your garments and accessories professionally. Stylists, image consultants and costume designers all have one thing in common: their closets are organized. Position your clothing by item, color, size, season, and outfit; any of these methods will help you keep track of things more easily. You can find multi-purpose closet organizers online and at stores like Target (Zellers in Canada) or Bed, Bath & Beyond in the US and Canada, or IKEA, with stores in 40 countries. They all offer affordable storage solutions for small spaces. Look for things that hang with shelves, drawers or pockets. These will free up space for your more precious commodities.

Plastic is a no-no

Try to avoid using plastic of any kind, especially garment bags or the dry cleaner's plastic covers. Plastic doesn't let the clothing breathe and traps any moisture, which can lead to smells or mildew. It's best to store your better clothes in cloth garment bags or acid-free boxes. Elizabeth Mason, founder of The Paper Bag Princess, a store specializing in designer vintage and couture clothes, suggests draping clothing with a cotton sheet as a stopgap by cutting a hole in the middle of the sheet for the hanger.

If you do use plastic storage bins, carefully cover the sides and bottom with acid-free tissue paper, but don't seal up the container; instead cover it with white cotton or muslin to keep out the dust. Acid-free means the paper has a neutral pH and is recommended by experts and curators who specialize in preserving textiles and clothing. Acid-free tissue is available in flat sheets or rolls in a variety of sizes and helps prevent discoloration and decay of garments. When folding or layering garments for box storage, you'll ensure longevity if you use acid-free boxes and acid-free, unbuffered tissue paper. Acid-free papers and boxes are readily available – check the internet for your nearest supplier.

Bust the dust

Keeping dust out of the closet and off the clothes is just as important as preventing moths from devouring your precious silks and woolens. Regardless of whether your clothing is valuable vintage couture or not, it pays to have some preventive measures in place. While using natural cedar blocks or lavender sachets may help prevent moths from dining on your fibers in unsealed closets, chests and drawers, the concentration of these phyto fumes isn't lethal enough to guarantee results.

Vacuum your closet from top to bottom several times a year and make a habit of closing the closet door when not in use, not only as a precaution to keep pests out, but also to block out light. Light fades and ages fabric. Moths will eat any animal-based material including felt and feathers. Vacuuming regularly also picks up lint, pet hair and other debris the larvae can feed on. Doris Raymond, owner of The Way We Wore, keeps her collection of coquettish chapeaus out in the open, but maintains a cleaning regimen. "I use a small vacuum cleaner, one with a wand and small tip. It doesn't cause stress to the materials." When you bring your new finds home, make sure to brush (preferably outside) or vacuum them gently but thoroughly, and don't integrate them into your regular clothing for a few days.

Some vintage clothing experts recommend placing woolens in plastic and sticking them in the freezer overnight so that the freezing cold can kill any moth eggs or larvae. Cold storage is a popular method for storing fur and leather coats. It can't hurt, but cold storage facilities often treat their vaults with pest-controlling substances, so none of these methods is a fail-safe by itself.

To hang or not to hang

To hang or not to hang... that wasn't a problem for medieval monarchs. But having the right kind of hanger is very important, so immediately recycle all wire hangers or those large plastic hangers that come in a rainbow of colors. Those short, straight, satin padded hangers are pretty, but please use with discretion unless you drape them with acid-free tissue, and only then for sleeveless garments or lingerie. Remember the shoulder of the garment is likely to adapt to the shape of the hanger over time, creating an unsightly bulge and stretching the fabric, altering the way the item will fit and look. Fibers can stretch, and older fibers fray and break.

The weight of the garment pulls on the shoulder or top of the item, and weakens the fabric overall. Clothes with strong construction, including coats, blazers, suit jackets, skirts – as well as fabrics that wrinkle or crush easily like silk, velvet and satin – are all candidates for the right hanger. One that seems to have the seal of approval from several dealers of 20th-century couture is a widely available lightweight, velvety smooth flocked and ultra thin space-saving hanger such as the ones made by the company Real Simple Solutions® and many others.

✓ QUICK HANGER CHECKLIST

If the answer to any of the following questions is yes, then folding or storing flat is the best way to go.

- Is the item a knit?
- Is the item heavy or weighty but not a coat, constructed jacket or dress?
- Is the item older, or made with a more delicate fabric such as silk, velvet or taffeta?

A cedar-lined drawer helps protect against moths.

Folding clothing has minor challenges; you need to lay sheets of acid-free tissue between the layers for items you don't wear often. Avoid sharp folds if it's a tightly woven fabric, as these could cause a breakdown of the fabric over time. Rolling softer or thicker pieces helps prevent wrinkles and makes it easier to find things without disturbing everything around them.

Not all roads lead to Rome

Once upon a time there were no dry cleaners. In ancient Rome, the local laundromat was called a *fullonica*; *fullo* is someone who washes cloth. A substance we call Fuller's earth (a clay-like mineral substance) was used to remove lanolin and other greasy by-products from wool to grass. While we no longer do as the Romans do, many consumers still rely on others to do the laundry, often a dry cleaner.

Workers putting up clothes for drying: a Roman fresco of the fullonica of Veranius Hypsaeus in Pompeii.

Dry cleaning isn't really dry. It's simply a cleaning process that substitutes a chemical solvent for water to clean the clothing. As early as 1821, a tailor named Thomas Jenning, the first African American to receive a patent, invented the "dry-scouring" process. Around the same time period, a Frenchman named Jean Baptiste Jolly, who dyed textiles for a living, discovered a similar modus operandi when kerosene was accidentally spilled on some cloth.

Madame Paulette, a cleaner and restorer of fine fabrics in New York City for over fifty years, specializes in handling couture and vintage garments. When the Metropolitan Museum of Art in New York City was preparing an exhibition of Coco Chanel, they turned to Madame Paulette. Many experts, though, express caution when sending precious couture garments to the dry cleaners as not all cleaners are as experienced as Madame Paulette. John Madessian, president of Madame Paulette, agrees. "It's not worth taking a chance if a dry cleaner isn't known for specialty work. People don't know about us unless they're connoisseurs, but we can evaluate things from a digital photograph."

Madame Paulette offers a free, virtual evaluation that begins with sending them an image via email. The cost of the actual work depends on what they find and is determined on a case-by-case basis. But just knowing you could send your precious Poiret to these "heads of thread" takes a bit of the worry out of collecting, wearing and spilling on couture clothing. Pioneers in the technology of preservation and restoration, Madame Paulette developed a

technique using black light to detect stains invisible to the naked eye. They can restore things others would find unsalvageable. For example, the original colors on Pucci prints tended to bleed. According to Madessian, Puccis are sensitive to water. "It's a tricky thing, but we can remove the fugitive dyes that have bled and add, not color, but the vibrancy and sheen that fades over time."

1947 Dior cocktail dress. Anything Dior is highly collectible and should be cared for accordingly.

Spot be gone

When the article of clothing you've managed to find has a noticeable stain, you should pass on it. Usually if a garment at resale is sporting a stain, it has probably already set in the fabric. However, for those undaunted by a challenge and the risk of damaging the item further, one trick for testing something is to dab a cotton ball or swab in a liquid stain remover and press it gently into the selvage of an inside seam or hem to test for color fastness. If dye is visible on the cotton, abandon the mission and blot with a clean, dry, white cloth to absorb any moisture from the cleaning solution.

If you don't see dye, look to see if the fabric changed in any way after the cleaning solution dried. Any noticeable results like rings or puckers aren't good. Should you be the perpetrator of a spill or spot, act quickly. Scrape off any solids with a spoon or dull-edged knife. Elizabeth Mason says, "I spot clean, brush and steam the clothing. Older fabrics are more fragile and require gentle handling. Do your color test; if you think the fabric can handle cool water, pat – but don't rub – a bit of cold or room temperature water onto the spot to dilute or dissolve the stain." Old-fashioned recipes for removing stains have proven effective over the years. For example, a paste of baking soda, salt and water can remove tough-to-get-out perspiration rings from certain fabrics like cotton and linen.

Don't leave the store without it

When shopping in person, always inspect the goods before you leave the store. It's advisable to do this before you bring it up to the cash register. Clearly, if you know the dealer, should you find a flaw such as a stain, you may be able to work something out. If you purchased something on eBay that arrived with a stain or odor not referenced in the item's auction description, you have several options, including contacting the seller directly regarding your concern. Established online sites like eBay are driven by buyer's reviews. In order to avoid a negative review, most reputable sellers will work with you. eBay has a 'Help' section which is thorough when it comes to resolving buying problems. For other online purchases, look for or ask about their return policy and guarantees. PayPal has a protocol for protesting a purchase and requesting a refund, so consider paying via PayPal for protection in the case of unwanted surprises.

Repairs and emergencies

To help fix anything beyond the simplest of repairs, you need to go to specialists. If your coveted garment has a recognizable label like Chanel or Valentino, you might consider contacting their closest boutique. Kathy Davoudi-Gohari, a Regional Manager with Valentino in Beverly Hills, frequently shares restoration and cleaning resources with owners and sometimes can assist, for a fee, with repairs of Valentino garments.

Reweaving can fix flaws like moth holes, small tears and cigarette burns in sweaters and knits. Larger tears call for inweaving, which uses a patch of fabric cut from a hidden part of the garment, such as a hem. Reknitting involves knitting hidden strands from sweaters and knits into the damaged area. Know in advance that repairs like these might still be visible, although much less noticeable. To find the best resources and experts in your area, try online city listings like CitySearch (www.citysearch.com) or Yelp (www.yelp.com) in the United States. Qype (www.qype.co.uk) is a similar user-generated review site available in Europe, the Middle East and Asia, with listings in over 150 countries. Consider contacting auction houses that specialize in textiles; or regional theatre troupes, ballet companies or costume rental companies, since they work with costumes and clothing that need regular maintenance. To handle small emergencies, like reattaching a button or a sewing up a small seam opening, costume designers and stylists in Hollywood have what's called a "kit," stocked with lots of remedies for emergencies like stains, loose buttons and ripped seams. You can easily build your own mini-kit to handle simple fixes.

 CHECKLIST: INSTANT KIT

- Lint brush
- Soft Bristle brush
- Suede cleaning sponge
- Needle and thread
- Invisible thread
- Double-stick tape
- Safety pins
- Wipes
- Clothing steamer (if you have the space)

Steamers

It is worthwhile to invest in a professional steamer, not to be confused with lightweight travel steamers. Professional steamers with a pole and long flexible wand are readily available online or at deep discounters including Costco in the US and the UK. In Europe, look for a Carrefour. Steamers are easy to use and do the best job of freshening up tired, wrinkled clothing without leaving creases or the risk of burning from a too-hot iron. Steaming can also be helpful in fading musty odors from garments. The first time you use one, though, practice on machine-washable items to get the hang of it, as sometimes steamers can spit or drip a bit. However, most clothing will respond beautifully to an occasional steaming.

Lint brush

A lint brush is essential. The long-handled ones with a velvety side that will catch pet hair and everything else will last forever. It's important to brush your sturdier clothing, particularly coats, after each wearing. You should also brush the shoulders of clothing that has hung in a closet without being worn for a year or more as there might be an accumulation of dust. This dust buildup can damage and fade fabric, ruining a garment for future wear.

Wipes

For the clothes that are dry-cleaned or regularly laundered in a washing machine (including your contemporary and sturdier purchases like a trench coat or blazer), you can add hand wipes to the formula. Keep in mind that this suggestion may not work on older fabrics that are delicate as the chemicals may be too harsh. Popular with stylists and set costumers on photo shoots, TV and movie sets, hand wipes have been successfully used to remove lightweight spots and dirt marks. Look for a wipe with alcohol in the list of ingredients, as many brands of wipes don't use alcohol in their formulas, which acts as the cleaning agent. Hand wipes like Wet Ones do include alcohol in most of their wipes. Alcohol also evaporates quickly, which speeds up the drying process on damp fabric. Shout® detergent markets a wipe that uses enzymes to lift and absorb stains, and works particularly well on oily residues, but the main cleaning agent is a form of alcohol. The difference between a hand wipe and a detergent wipe is that hand wipes are safe to use on the body, and detergent wipes are to be used only for removing stains and spots from colorfast clothing. The method is the same for both types of wipes. Just pat the spot, stain or spill gently, don't rub aggressively, and allow to air dry.

 TIP

Always air out your clothing for a day after wearing it before you return it to your closet or drawer. This helps prevent smells from smog, smoke, perspiration and food getting too attached and spreading to your other clothing.

Look for a wipe with alcohol in the list of ingredients

 TIP

Janie Bryant, the costume designer for the hit AMC show *Mad Men* (a period drama set in the early 1960s), keeps a spray bottle of vodka and water. A few spritzes will get rid of perfume or body odors.

With the right amount of preparation and effort, you can manage the maintenance of your vintage couture finds or your everyday favorites. After making your investment in these special garments, you want to be able to enjoy them for years and even decades to come.

The collectors

06

The collectors

"Elegance is refusal." Vogue editor and collector extraordinaire Diana Vreeland in an interview with Christopher Hemphill before her death.

The one common denominator that all the collectors profiled here have in common is elegance. However, if Diana Vreeland's quote about elegance is to be taken literally, then one might ask, what exactly is being refused? After some thought the answer emerges; it is the refusal to accept limitations and convention.

The steadfast determination and enthusiasm expressed by the collector is apparent. Notably all those interviewed for the book began our conversations identically. "I just found this great piece, you'll never believe how much I paid for it." Their enthusiasm was unrestrained and infectious. Seeking out a rare and beautiful couture item at an affordable price can be a time-consuming and challenging endeavor. This treasure-hunting exercise never daunted any of the collectors we met.

This book will aid novice and pro alike in their quest to find the rare and beautiful piece. However, a collecting lifestyle is in part the lesson learned from the collectors profiled here. Free time is devoted to finding treasures and stocking them away for a later day. This collecting way of life seems to come naturally to those who practice it, like breathing in and out.

It is said, "the past is an orchestra the present conducts." This is especially true about the art of haute couture. Collectors around the globe are preserving a piece of the past while incorporating it into and celebrating the present.

Lorrie Ivas

01

Since I have devoted my life to fashion – both in livelihood and lifestyle – the word "shopping" doesn't evoke tedium but inspiration – not for the new, but for the unique. Realizing my most comfortable go-to pieces of black leggings and turtlenecks create a great foundation for a 1950s leopard jacket ($25/£14/€20), or a 1960s sculpted Balenciaga-like coat ($30/£16/€24), I found true bliss in never seeing anyone else in my outfits, and never having an outstanding credit card balance!

My love of 20th-century fashions naturally blends with my love of teaching – Fashion Trends and Design, Fashion History, Retail Merchandising, Advertising and Display. I not only collect clothes and accessories, but rare fashion magazines and books as well.

There is nothing in my wardrobe where I don't find inspiration... a memory of its "capture" or the places I've already worn it. Living in perfect Southern California beachfront weather affords little need for winter gear, but that doesn't stop my search for unique coats and

Collector Lorrie Ivas in her living room with her favorite leopard jacket.

ornamented cardigans, whether Lilli Ann, Bonnie Cashin, Chanel and Hollywood's Irene, or unknown labels from New Orleans to Pittsburgh. The 1930s onward produced some of the most colorful details, textures, and silhouettes, all able to be "transported" to the 21st century with my simple black leggings, turtleneck, flats or heels.

Anyone can spend exorbitant amounts on clothing. It necessitates no inherent style to spend $7000 (£3800/€5500) on an ensemble, but spending $7 (£3.80/€5.50)... now that's creativity! Any sales associate worthy of their commission will match you with costly pieces-of-the-moment. But are they your style? *US Weekly*'s "Who Wore it Best?" or Joan Rivers' "Bitch Stole My Look" on Fashion Police remind me that you are never entirely unique when purchasing something current. The dreaded social scandal of "two women in the same dress" gets voracious media coverage. So $7000 (£3800/€5500) really didn't buy anyone exclusivity. But a vintage garment, selected from a quality emporium to the random garage sale, guarantees it.

Lorrie's favorite couture coats are displayed on dress forms as art.

My dream shopping trips include Paris and London, but a road trip across the USA, scouring tag sales and quaint thrift stores in city outskirts, is on my to-do list. Walking down Madison or Fifth Avenues in NYC and shopping the "B's" – Bergdorf-Goodman, Henri Bendel, Barneys, Bloomingdales – is a beloved exercise I do two times a year – for pleasure and research. Where I truly enjoy spending money, though, is at the Manhattan charity shops – City Opera Thrift, the multiple Housing Works, and the Sloan-Kettering Thrift Store. Paris is a longer trip, but has great high-end vintage and locales with more affordable finds, including Mouton à Cinq Pattes, and the Marché aux Puces St-Ouen de Clignancourt.

I do not have a "vintage clothing" body. Translation: last century's women were more delicately boned, anthropologically

Vintage wool and cashmere Geoffrey Beene dresses.

(Left) 1975 Mouton green wool jacket, a Paris flea market find. (Far left) One of Lorrie's favorite pieces is this fabulous Jean Paul Gaultier dragon wool jacket from a local Los Angeles thrift shop.

speaking. Garments had shorter back-waist lengths and smaller armholes. Dresses from bygone eras have an empire waist on me. Jackets make me look like an organ grinder's monkey – too short sleeves – too short everything! That's when shears come into play. Long sleeves become three-quarter. Two of my favorite skirts ($18/£10/€14 and $15/£8/€12) were once dresses – now creatively beheaded to fit my 5'10" (178 cm) frame. Bodices become vests or supply waistband fabric. The same for styles a bit too long, with unglamorous "armpit" stains, or surviving "moth and cigarette wars" where holes and burn marks abound, lowering prices. I see these as challenges to correct, camouflage or redesign and, if beyond wear, they become a scarf, shawl or chair pillow.

Charity vintage/resale shops are weekly destinations on my shopping route. The Colleagues shop in Santa Monica (supporting The Children's Institute), run by amazing women who donate their time and wardrobes, are a major source of my most favored Mugler, Givenchy, Beene and Gaultier. They remind me how fashion brings joy and philanthropy. Talk about guilt-less shopping! The same goes for The American Cancer Society's Discovery Shops (Martin Margiela blazer for $11/£6/€9). Philanthropically spending on sustainable vintage is the new "green." Giving to charity begins at home and, in my case, my closet. Next routine – weekend yard sales, church bazaars and flea markets. A recent excursion brought a 1958 cocktail ensemble for $5/£3/€4, sold by the owner's daughter, which opened a dialogue of cherished memories of our stylish mothers. Doris Day, my favorite, could have worn it in *Pillow Talk* (1959). Hollywood's effect on fashion is obvious, and living near film studios, one can buy garments divested from warehouses. Costume designers and stylists also cull personal inventory at tag sales.

Collect what you love, not what you think will be valuable. Seeing a revered painting hanging on a gallery wall reminds me that

1960s vintage couture "beheaded" dress and 1950s wool sweater, in preparation for an update and adjustment for fit.

my art hangs as well, but on a rod aided by hangers and dress forms. I curate my closet. When reading *Art Forum*, new artists are discovered; when reading fashion magazines, designers' inspirations from the past are evident. Picasso and Dali are priceless, but McCardell, Kamali, Alaïa, Karan, Beene and Gaultier make my day. So do screen fashion icons Lauren Bacall, Audrey Hepburn, Mary Tyler Moore and costume designers today, especially Patricia Field – genius at mixing vintage with new.

How wonderful to change the mundane task of daily dressing into a creative moment. No journal keeping for me. I wear my journal. When selecting an outfit, I recall where I found it and tell friends who truly understand the joy of scoring a $2 (£1/€1.60) Diesel top, or the $3 (£1.63/€2.36) TSE harem pants. And to those pieces still hanging in my closet, inspiring me but perhaps not yet worn... I banish the closet organizers' mantra, "If you haven't worn it in two years, toss it!" Toss it? Those pieces are reminders of adventure to come... and when it comes, that is when they will be worn. "Shop your closet" is not a recessionary phrase but building/remodeling a wardrobe – a constant work in progress. As fine wine increases in value with age, so does my wardrobe.

A mix of embellished designer cardigans and current Barneys black silk skirt create an interesting and highly original style.

Joanne Stillman

02

I guess one could say my love of fashion started when I was a little girl. The biggest influence in my life was my Aunt Betty. I spent my summers with her in Philadelphia where she taught me the art of "collecting."

My aunt was a true style maven. She taught me her secret of mixing high-end couture with bargain basement finds. At a time when consignment shops were considered a place for the needy, my aunt would avidly shop them without a second thought. Her philosophy of fashion and style, as well as life, was to follow what inspires you, not what the "Joneses" think. She would take me along on these fun and adventurous hunts for style and fashion. This was the greatest gift she could give me and it has lead to my lifelong passion for seeking out fashion at a bargain price.

Finding that ultimate piece, whether it is a shirt, hat, or a pair of

Collector Joanne Stillman advises wearing black opera gloves for a touch of glamour – even during the day: "I always love to feel like a diva."

shoes, is the thrill of collecting. Fashion is my art world; finding a vintage Madame Grès at an estate sale is my version of finding an unknown work by Rousseau. Growing up in Los Angeles, this hunt was relatively easy. Since moving to Philadelphia where my lessons were taught, the pursuit has got more challenging. It is this challenge that has brought me full circle.

Since moving to the suburbs of Philadelphia, I have a new appreciation for discovering hidden treasures. Driving through the countryside and coming upon an odd shop, reminiscent of the past, and finding a vintage Lilli Ann black, three-quarter sleeve, mink collar swing coat makes the purchase all the better. This beautiful piece of clothing has a rebirth and will be worn proudly with a Vera Wang cocktail dress, as well as with a basic pair of black leggings and turtleneck. When on the prowl for that perfect jacket, nothing goes unnoticed. I might be looking for a jacket, but my eye is always searching for that inspirational gem.

Joanne's favorite collection of beaded and embroidered skirts.

This is a collection of some of Joanne's beautiful evening dresses.

My collection is ever-growing and I am always on the hunt, even in my closet. You never know what you may have stored, forgotten about, or misplaced. I find the most amazing pieces at yard sales and thrift stores at prices that would knock your socks off. Just the other day I purchased a beautiful vintage straw handbag embellished with pink silk roses for $2 (£1/€1.60). Voila, my new summer go-to bag was in hand! When I peruse the thrift stores, I have to dig deep and keep an open mind. At first glance, one might think there is nothing worth purchasing and all of a sudden, there it is a simple white blouse with strange-looking sleeves. I see beyond the odd-shaped sleeves and imagine how that blouse would look sleeveless and I snatch up the blouse as if it were gold. I can't wait to get it home and doctor it up by cutting off those sleeves and trying it on with my oversized Martin Margiela wrap pants. I knew they would go together like bread and butter.

I think my aunt would be proud of me and elated that I am living and collecting as she did. I have an appreciation for, not just the labels, but also the canvas that envelops the form. The fabric is my canvas and the texture, print, and draperies are the paints. That is the charge that sparks my mind and keeps me on my toes. Collecting fashion is not a hobby or pastime, it is a lifestyle. This lifestyle has kept me going, no matter what happens, bad or good; my collection always puts a smile on my face.

A couture coat in a timeless style.

Beverly Soloman

03

My mother was a fashion designer and went to art school in Miami. As a child I used to study her sketches and spent a lot of time in her closet, looking at all the beautiful clothes and shoes. When I was six she started taking me shopping. She would turn a dress inside out to show me the seams and darts, and point out the workmanship, explaining the difference between a good dress and a cheap dress.

Those early shopping expeditions were the impetus for me to choose a career in beauty and fashion, and as a result I became a collector of couture and designer clothing and accessories.

My first designer purchase was an Oscar de la Renta necklace, not haute couture, but accessories are the gateway to the real thing, and the designers were adding to their cachet and accessibility with accessories like shoes, belts, bags and jewelry. I still have that necklace, along with most of the best acquisitions I've made over the years.

Working in high-end department stores, starting with my first

(Above) Beverly Soloman with some of her favorite vintage purses. (Right) Beverly in a wonderful tribal print outfit.

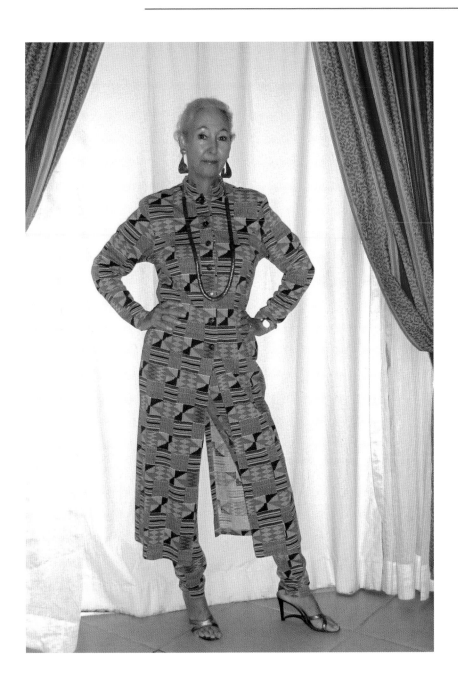

few jobs when I was in high school, I cultivated relationships that provided access to the best clothes at the best prices. I knew everybody and when things would go on sale, I was one of the first ones to know about it. I've had a great Chanel blouse and a jacket from one of Armani's first collections all these years. If you take good care of things, they last.

A friend who shopped at a fancy boutique started inviting me to the owner's private sales of the remnants from the sale rack, marked down so many times, the owner finally had to practically give them away. I didn't frequent the shop on a regular basis, so there were always interesting things. Acquisitions from that time period in my life include a Bill Blass jacket and an Oscar de la Renta blouse.

I live on a ranch outside of Austin, Texas. There are a lot of wealthy enclaves on the lakes and rivers in this area. We don't have Goodwill stores here; instead, there are small, local charity shops scattered about. My husband Pablo is a sculptor and he's always looking for unusual things to incorporate into his art. About ten years ago, we wandered into one of these places. While I was waiting for him to check the place out, I rummaged through a basket of scarves. I still get chills when I think about finding a Hermès scarf, worth about $300 (£163/€236), for one dollar. Since then, scarves have become my addiction. I paid $3 (£1.63/€2.36) for a Chanel scarf, the most valuable one in my collection.

We go to France every year. I have to travel light but I need to look fashionable. I wear a uniform of black jeans and black cashmere sweaters. I keep it simple with something like a good gold cuff bracelet, but I always have my scarves.

I'm often mistaken for a Parisian. The French compliment you on wearing the same thing over and over. They are more interested in how you look and feel in your clothes. Since we usually go in the fall or winter, I don't leave without an Armani collarless car coat I picked up for $135 (£73/€106) in the early 1980s that was originally priced at $800 (£434/€630). I buy less now. When I was young I bought things I wanted; now I edit based on how the thing will fit into my existing wardrobe, but I ask myself if I will wear it or cherish it. Couture and designer clothing is often just another form of art.

Beverly with her
scarf collection.

Lisa Berman

04

My family is from Ohio, and coming from the Midwest we were accustomed to antiques and being surrounded by items from the past. We're a family that makes handcrafted things; it's our heritage. When my mother and her cousin were growing up, they would look at fashion magazines and point out details of dresses they liked to their grandmother. She would roll out a bolt of fabric on the kitchen table and, without a chalk line, could look at the two girls and cut out dresses. My great grandmother, along with my grandmother, designed and constructed my entire wardrobe. She was our home haute couturier. I thought a grandmother who created beautiful clothing was normal, until I was transplanted to Laguna Beach. Shopping for a new Southern California wardrobe I realized I had actually been wearing what was considered couture clothing.

Lisa Berman in her atelier wearing a red wool custom-made couture piece.

Lisa wearing
her favorite
Lanvin cocktail
dress with her
portrait.

My mother had her own action sportswear company called Instant
Reactions in the mid-1970s, so I grew up going to the California
Market Center, as it's called today, home to wholesale showrooms for
retail buyers.

My mother loved Norma Kamali so, of course, I was wearing
Kamali, and whatever designer clothing I could sneak out of the
house, including Zandra Rhodes. I still have a few of my mother's
pieces.

This tradition has carried on through the birth of my daughter
in 2008. My husband complained about her boring baby clothes and
an artist, whose work I showed in the gallery I owned at the time,
showed up with an entire trousseau of handmade silk dupioni
dresses and diaper covers, all hand embroidered.

My collection is very eclectic and diverse, primarily focused on accessories. I'm not a Chanel girl. A former roommate once tried to pay the rent with a Chanel suit, but instead I took her Hervé Leger pants. One piece of advice I would pass along to budding collectors is: It pays to have a relationship with a good tailor. You can use any dry cleaner's tailoring services for basic hems, but try to find a serious tailor for serious alterations. One tailor I knew would end up with these fabulous clothes because sometimes people never picked up their garments. He once gave me a Gianfranco Ferré suit I still have today.

Issey Mayake suit displayed on a mannequin.

Lisa has her "sculpture to wear" jewelry displayed in cases alongside a unique paper lace shawl.

I've found some incredible things at garage sales, including a Schiaparelli hat for $3 (£1.63/€2.36). One incredible find was a Rudi Gernreich topless swimsuit. Can you imagine! I bought the Gernreich swimsuit at a garage sale for only $8 (£4.34/€6.30). In 2008, a similar suit sold for $2000 (£1085/€1574) at a Christie's auction.

I try not to buy things with stains or obvious flaws, but if damaged and irresistible, I consider can it be covered with a brooch or belt? One exception was a couple of unwearable Thierry Mugler suits I bought to make patterns from.

I use an amazing enzyme-based carpet and upholstery cleaner called Wow Green for difficult stains. I've had a lot of success using this product to remove new stains and spots, in particular on handbags.

Gina and Sasha Cassavetes

05

I first became aware of fashion when I left the San Fernando Valley and moved to Hollywood in 2006, only to discover the sweatshirt and hoodie look was clearly not working in the city!

I learned the real lessons of fashion when I was hired at Marc Jacobs. Working for a company that is so passionate about fashion and allows for variation and individuality forces you to find out what you like and who you are (in terms of fashion).

During the two years I worked in the retail department I found my collection naturally flourished. The more knowledge I would gain on different designers, their collections, personality and style options, the more precious clothing became and worthy of collecting.

I am part of a family of actors, writers and directors. I observed their creativity and took it all in. My father, Nick Cassavetes, used to tell me it's important to have one nice watch, one nice pair of sunglasses, and one nice pair of shoes. I like that. I still need to work on the watch. My glamorous grandmother, Gena Rowlands, has

fabulous jewelry and I cherish the pieces she's given me. I think we all love accessories; they pull everything together.

My first item of collectible couture was a hand-me-down from my stylish stepmother. She gave me a pair of Yves Saint Laurent knee-high boots that had never been worn. Black suede with a delicate bow that wraps around the top of the boot, accentuating my hamstring muscle, they were and still are my favorite sexy boots. Currently I am addicted to another pair of her hand-me-down boots by Balenciaga.

When I travel I always try to find the hot consignment, vintage and secondhand stores. I've found some amazing pieces. I found a beautiful Juicy Couture dress for $40 (£22/€31), Balenciaga sunglasses for $95 (£52/€75), and some Marc Jacobs pink suede boots for $100 (£54/€79). If you go out with your eyes open it's amazing what you will find. The most unexpected place I found something great was in an ex-boyfriend's closet. He had all these really rare vintage tee shirts that didn't fit him anymore so he let me

Gina wearing a great Marc Jacobs dress with suede Manolo Blahnik boots. Both pieces purchased at local designer outlet stores for a fraction of their original price. Sasha wearing on of her favorite finds.

A few great finds: Marc Jacobs red patent ski boots and Betsey Johnson silver spider jacket.

have at it. It helps to have friends and family who love to shop as eventually they'll need to make some room for their new finds. You can tempt them with a chunk of change or even offer to run an errand or help out with some busy work. Be open to trading, as a lot of people who shop are also people who love to trade.

My sister Sacha is my roommate and we collect together. She's a make-up artist; she's amazingly visual and has a real knack for putting things together in interesting ways. She likes to mix couture with funky stuff, torn-up jeans, boxers and boots. She gets her best stuff in secondhand stores outside of major cities; she takes the time to shop in far-flung places. She's got couture radar!

For people just starting out my suggestion would be, go for basics. Wait till you have a few wearable things before you splurge on a crazy outfit you might only wear once. You will always need your basics, important things like a great pair of jeans, a nice black pea coat, a cashmere sweater, or a little black dress with some sexy heels.

A beaded gold vintage couture piece that these sisters found on one of their flea market shopping excursions. Sasha recommends visiting antique malls outside of major cities to get the best deals.

Susan Dalgliesh

06

Underneath the brocade jacket, Susan is wearing an Issey Miyake silver dress. "The sleeves are so long they cover my hands, but that's what I like about it. Exotic materials and unusual designs appeal to me."

I've been buying designer and couture clothes in London since I was 13. Recycling fashion has always appealed to me, so I only go to thrift stores or charity shops, where the money goes to a good cause. Clothes that are unique, especially if the materials are exotic in some way, interest me the most. Over the years I've learned to identify quality. High-end designer and couture clothing has a different look and feel. If you want to wear the clothing, it's important to only buy things that appeal to you. In my teens, I wore beaded dresses from the 1920s. Then I just naturally moved through the decades.

I'm fond of Galliano's early work from the 80s and I like Comme des Garçons from this same time period because it's really strange. Lately I'm wearing dresses by Miss Mouse. She wasn't a couturier, but she had a store on King's Road in the 70s and made a lot of custom stuff for her pop star friends.

I live on a boat outside central London, and I had special cabinets lined with cedar built. The good stuff is on padded hangers and I use acid-free tissue to wrap a few things. Several years ago, before I moved to the boat, half of my wardrobe was lost due to a moth infestation. It was devastating. So far, moths haven't been a problem. But on the boat, water could ruin everything.

During a discussion with my son about my assets, I showed him the clothing I thought was valuable. Things I wouldn't want him to give away. He started adding up the total and we realized the lot was worth a large sum of money. That's when I decided to insure my clothing. My insurance agent added an extra contents provision, over and above the usual coverage, that includes water damage.

My favorite pieces include a Balenciaga suit that no one but me likes. Nobody comments when I wear it, it's very minimal with an interesting cut, but it's worth thousands of pounds. I've been called an anorak, British slang for someone who is obsessively interested in something that no one else cares about.

My strategy is to buy clothes from a decade or style that is fading or last year's fad. Recently I started picking up stuff by a cult designer from the late 90s whose popularity was brief. Yesterday's fashions, even if they are high quality, can be had for very little money. When things start to look uncool and jarring to the eye, just put them away for ten years. Their moment comes when the decade or style recycles and their value starts to jump.

(Below left) This vintage floral number is my favorite dress and is almost flawless on the inside. Behind my chair is an oyster-colored evening coat with an embroidered disc by Bill Gibbs.

(Below right) A classic red jacket.

Deborah Woolf

07

Deborah is a huge Jean Muir fan; she owns and wears a lot of her clothes from the 1960s. This is an early 1960s suede mini featuring Muir's trademark punch-cut suede. Deborah likes to imagine Anita Pallenberg or Marianne Faithful wearing a dress like this back then.

I've been collecting quite seriously for over 30 years, since I was about 13. My collection goes up to the 1970s, but there are some things by Vivienne Westwood, Jean Paul Gaultier and a few of the Japanese designers that are from the 80s. Up and coming designers, as well as novelty prints and quirky items, appeal to me. But what really attracts me is the tailoring in the item, the craft and skill of the designer.

As a teenager, I felt savvy when I would pick up vintage at jumble sales. Back then; we called vintage stuff "secondhand." You can still find great vintage in the street markets and at charity shops.

London department store sales and bargain basements used to be good – with proper mark-down prices – especially during the last day of the sale. It was amazing what I could find! These days it's a different story; often the best stuff isn't included in the sale so I find I don't shop from them much now.

After leaving school I worked in TV, films, commercials and music videos and became a senior creative at MTV UK. Styling and

set design projects were part of my assignments during those years, which dovetailed nicely with my love of shopping for and collecting vintage and couture clothing.

I took a sabbatical from MTV and started doing vintage fairs to sell some of my collection. When I was still at school, I'd had a Sunday market stall to sell some of my finds. Releasing things from my collection is necessary but always painful!

The V&A Museum asked me to supply vintage clothing for the gift shop they were planning during 'The Golden Age of Couture Paris and London 1947-57' exhibition in the fall of 2007. That's when things started to take off, and I opened Deborah Woolf Vintage. But first and foremost I am a collector; I'm not a resale shop or dress agency, I

don't take things on commission or buy in bulk; I still handpick everything.

Just thinking about picking one favorite thing from my collection is hard; there's so much to choose from. One of my treasured items, which isn't couture, is a Jean Muir mini suede dress from the 60s. A 70s fave is a Biba faux leopard print jacket in the true Glam Rock style. All the male pop stars from that era like Marc Bolan and Brian Eno were seen wearing this signature Biba-style jacket with their platform shoes and skinny flared pants.

The key to collecting is to only buy what you like. If you can't wear something because it's too small or too delicate, put it on display; that way you'll always enjoy it.

Where to shop

07

Where to shop: city guides

"I shop therefore I am"
Barbara Kruger

S hopping is not a destination, but rather a journey. When shopping for vintage and resale garments, remember that there is never a wasted visit. Every visit allows you to expand your education by visually absorbing the taste level of that store's buyer when entering the store or clicking on their website or blog. You are able to view items from decades ago that have stood the test of time, seen eras mixed with other eras through the merchandising creativity of each proprietor, all from every corner of the globe. When shopping for yourself, not rushing to find something for a last-minute event, you are truly "building" your personal wardrobe. Success is when one can say, "I don't NEED any more clothing," but bliss is constantly exploring and adding the "spice" to an already secure selection.

Legend

DR – Designer Resale

V – Vintage

SD – Specialty Discount

SS – Specialty Store

William Vintage

The stores are listed by city in alphabetical order; the legend designates the type of merchandise that is carried by category such as vintage, designer resale, specialty discount store (offering designer discounted merchandise) or specialty store (usually with a parent establishment).

Los Angeles

Los Angeles is a mecca when it comes to shopping for everything from affordable couture to perusing gowns worn on the red carpet. Celebrities' closets provide a direct pipeline to the inventories of the top LA resale shops. Upscale retailers including Neiman Marcus, Saks Fifth Avenue and Barneys New York offer a plethora of top designer brands. With major sales scheduled throughout the year, it is definitely worth finding out when they are held. The premium outlet malls located within driving distance and specialty store sales all complement the vintage emporium treasure troves of this area.

Designer resale and vintage

The Address Boutique (DR)
1116 Wilshire Boulevard
Santa Monica, CA 90401
(1) 310 394 1406
www.theaddressboutique.com
addressboutique@earthlink.net

Owner Maureen Clavin has been in the business since 1963. She routinely visits the closets of recognizable names to stock her charming shop. Displayed by color, you'll find a mix of Prada, Cavalli, Gucci, Vera Wang, Chanel and Armani. Be sure to check out the section of superb separates and the sale rack.

The Address Boutique

Clothes Heaven (DR)
111 East Union Street
Pasadena, CA 91103
(1) 626 440 0929
www.clothesheaven.com
@ClothesHeaven

Nestled on a quaint side street in Pasadena since 1983, Clothes Heaven offers a sizable selection of European, American and Japanese designers including Gucci, Prada, Ann Demeulemeester, Donna Karan, Michael Kors, Issey Miyake and Yohji Yamamoto. Larayne Brannon, the proprietor, specializes in Chanel, and maintains a deep inventory of all things Coco. Coveted couture handbags are in every nook and cranny. Everything in the back saleroom is half off the regular resale price, and there's a bonus rack of goodies, all marked $29 (£15/€23) each.

Clothes
Heaven

The Colleagues (V & DR)
3312 Pico Boulevard
Santa Monica, CA 90405
(1) 310 396 7349
http://thecolleagues.com
info@thecolleagues.com

The Colleagues is a non-profit charity organization run by a small group of women since 1950. Their philosophy, "Philanthropy through Fashion," has raised millions to support the Children's Institute Inc., helping save LA children exposed to abuse. The shop includes designer fashions donated from some of the best closets in town. Rare Beene, Blass, Dior, YSL, Adolfo and Galanos nestle in with Oscar, Akris, Chanel, Dolce & Gabbana and Gucci. Rows of designer shoes, cases of costume jewelry, furs, scarves and hats could be from the 1940s thru today, with the provenance equally as intriguing as the finds. Menswear is stocked with the same eye for quality. The range of prices can fit any budget, and watch for their special sales in March, June and December.

Decades and Decades Two.1 (V & DR)
8214 ½ Melrose Avenue
Los Angeles, CA 90046
(1) 323 655 0223
www.decadesinc.com
info@decades.com
@CameronDecades

Upstairs Downstairs is the theme at Decades and DecadesTwo.1
where Cameron Silver and Christos Garkinos are the men behind this
style destination. It's not unusual to see something by Jean Patou,
Schiaparelli, Vionnet or Galanos. Downstairs, Decades Two.1 has a
mix of contemporary couture and designer labels. Decades holds
trunk shows around the world and you can visit their shop-in-shop at
Dover Street Market in London.

Decades

Golyester (V)
136 S La Brea Avenue
Los Angeles, CA 90036
(1) 323 931 1339
www.facebook.com/pages/Golyester

Esther Ginsberg, the woman behind this landmark LA emporium, has amassed an amazing collection of vintage textiles, shoes, purses, and hats, along with clothing from every decade of the 20th century. A true collector in her own right, Esther has cultivated a following with like-minded stylish women, Hollywood stylists, costume designers, and all seeking individuality in dress. The store name says it all: "Golly, Esther"... this store is amazing.

Great Labels (DR)
1126 Wilshire Boulevard
Santa Monica, CA 90401
(1) 310 451 2277
www.greatlabels.com

Andrea Waters, proprietor of this wisely edited store, whose name describes it perfectly: "Great Labels carries such fresh designer shoes, handbags, jewelry and accessories that you can forget you are at a consignment shop." Extremely current items hang among desirable classics. Healthy reductions of 50 percent, then 75 percent off already great prices constantly rotate the stock, allowing one to stay on budget or be able to accrue more! Chanel, Louboutin, Dolce & Gabbana, Prada, JPG and more.

Lily et Cie (V & DR)
9044 Burton Way
Beverly Hills, CA 90211
(1) 310 724 5757
www.lilyetcie.com
info@lilyetcie.com

Secluded behind big shade trees, Lily et Cie is easy to miss. Once inside, you're greeted by a series of lavish, museum-style vignettes of the crème de la crème of haute couture, from Emanuel Ungaro, Patou, Lacroix and Chanel. Rita Watnick presides over a fiefdom of fashion's finest. Half of her colossal inventory of 20th-century haute couture has never been worn. One-of-a-kind creations by Madame Grès, Jean Dessès and Hubert de Givenchy stand, red carpet ready, along with a hefty hoard of jewels. It is suggested to call in advance to book an appointment.

Lily et Cie

The Paper Bag Princess (V & DR)
8818 West Olympic Boulevard
Beverly Hills, CA 90211
(1) 310 385 9036
www.thepaperbagprincess.com
www.facebook.com/pages/The-Paper-Bag-Princess-Vintage-Couture
@princesspaper

Stepping into Elizabeth Mason's store is like entering a fabulous
treasure trove of fashion. The massive store is an enchanting maze of
departments, with one entire room devoted to vintage bridal gowns
from designers including Azzedine Alaïa and Yves Saint Laurent. A
private salon holds the haute couture, available by appointment.
Select items are sold online at both eBay and 1st Dibs.com. Mason is
a certified appraiser and the author of two books on the subject,
Valuable Vintage and *The Rag Street Journal*.

Paper Bag Princess

PJ London (DR)

11661 San Vicente Boulevard
Los Angeles, CA 90049
(1) 310 826 4649
www.pjlondon.com
pjlondon@aol.com

PJ London

Located in the wealthy neighborhood of Brentwood, owner Phyllis
Davis, a former fashion stylist, has a small but focused selection of
cocktail dresses and wardrobe-building separates from contemporary
designers like Stella McCartney and Dries van Noten, as well as Dolce
& Gabbana, Fendi and Dior. She also carries a great range of desirable
shoes, purses and jewelry. Things go on sale four times a year – at 60
percent off regular resale prices – in January, April, July and October.

The Way We Wore (V & DR)
334 S. La Brea Avenue
Los Angeles, CA 90036
(1) 323 937 0878
www.thewaywewore.com
thewaywewore@sbcglobal.net
@TheWayWeWoreLA

The Way We Wore has over a million pieces of vintage, designer and couture clothing going back to the 18th century. Founded by connoisseur Doris Raymond in 2004, the first floor of this colorful and whimsical vintage boutique is arranged by era. Accessories galore vie for your attention while a trove of coveted couture and designer labels beckon from the upstairs loft. Catch their sales in January and July, but assorted items sprinkled around the store are marked 50 percent off.

The Way We Wore

Specialty discount and specialty

Barneys New York (SS)
9570 Wilshire Blvd.
Beverly Hills, CA 90210
(1) 310 276 4400
www.barneys.com
www.facebook.com/BarneysNY
@BarneysNY

While there are the usual sales at Barneys New York in Beverly Hills, the holy grail of affordable couture is to be had during their annual warehouse sale, where you'll find markdowns of 50 to 75 percent. This sale was originally held at a Santa Monica airport hangar, but is now headquartered in the LA Convention Center. Keep your eye out for their Purple Card promotions: gift cards are awarded with different levels of spending. For even more savings, check their three outlet locations approximately an hour to two away.

Barneys New York Outlet (SD)
Camarillo Premium Outlet
740 E. Ventura Boulevard, Suite 710
Camarillo, CA 93010
(1) 805 445 1123

Barneys New York Outlet (SD)
Desert Hills Premium Outlet
48400 Seminole Drive, Suite 128
Cabazon, CA 92230
(1) 951 849 1600

Barneys New York Outlet (SD)
Carlsbad Premium Outlet
5620 Paseo del Norte, Suite 100-D
Carlsbad, CA 92008
(1) 760 929 600

Last Call by Neiman Marcus (SD)
Camarillo Premium Outlet
740 E. Ventura Boulevard, Suite 1350
Camarillo, CA 93010
(1) 805 482 4273
www.lastcall.com
@LastCallNM

Last Call by Neiman Marcus (SD)
Desert Hills Premium Outlet
48400 Seminole Drive, Suite 720
Cabazon, CA 92230
(1) 951 922 9009

Pick up some Badgley Mischka, Balmain, Dolce & Gabbana, Donna Karan and other labels you love at up to 70 percent off regular retail prices. Watch for their Caravan sales of A-list labels that make the rounds of the various stores. Shop online or at either of their two greater Los Angeles stores in the Premium Outlet Mall locations (Premium Outlet Mall locations are listed in this section) situated about an hour outside of Los Angeles.

Loehmann's (SD)
333 S. La Cienega Boulevard
Los Angeles, CA 90048
(1) 310 659 0674
www.loehmanns.com
@Loehmanns

The Back Room at Loehmann's is the place to look for 30 to 65 percent off high-end designers like Calvin Klein, Donna Karan, Valentino, and Dolce & Gabbana. They have 40 stores in 11 of the US states. Check out the "It's This Week" on their website for additional discounts and promotions.

Nordstrom Rack (SD)

shop.nordstrom.com/c/nordstrom-rack

@nordstrom_rack

Visit one of five Nordstrom Rack stores in the Los Angeles vicinity. Savings of 55 to 75 percent off are the norm. Nordstrom Rack has a Fashion Rewards program to earn savings vouchers. Merchandise is generally from their main stores and gets deposited once a week to the discount venues; ask a sales person when that day is for first pick. The really great items tend to go fast, so the early bird does get the proverbial Blahnik.

Nordstrom Rack Burbank Empire Center (SD)

1601 North Victory Place

Burbank, CA 91502

(1) 818 478 2930

Nordstrom Rack Glendale Fashion Center (SD)

227 North Glendale Avenue

Glendale, CA 91206

(1) 818 240 2404

Nordstrom Rack Beverly Connection (SD)

100 North La Cienega Boulevard

Los Angeles, CA 90048

(1)323 602 0282

Nordstrom Rack Topanga (SD)

21490 Victory Boulevard

Woodland Hills, CA 91367

(1) 818 884 6771

Nordstrom Rack The Promenade at Howard Hughes Center (SD)

6081 Center Drive

Los Angeles, CA 90045

(1) 310 641 4046

Premium Outlet Malls (SD)

www.premiumoutlets.com
@premiumoutlets

Bursting with brands like Dolce & Gabbana, Dior, DKNY, Giorgio Armani, Gucci, Michael Kors, Salvatore Ferragamo, Versace and Yves Saint Laurent, Premium Outlet Malls are a one-stop shop for affordable designer goods. They have a Travel & Tourism office that offers a VIP discount to groups of 15 or more who contact the outlet in advance. Members of the Automobile Club of America (AAA) receive the VIP discount by simply visiting the mall management office and showing their membership card. Receive a VIP Coupon Book with each gift card purchased online. Two Premium Outlet Mall locations are about an hour outside of Los Angeles so take your pick.

Camarillo Premium Outlet (SD)
740 E. Ventura Boulevard
Camarillo, CA 93010
(1) 805 445 8520

Desert Hills Premium Outlet (SD)
48400 Seminole Drive
Cabazon, CA 92230
(1) 951 849 6641

Carlsbad Premium Outlet (SD)
5620 Paseo del Norte, Suite 100
Carlsbad, CA 92008
(1) 760 804 9000

Saks Fifth Avenue (SS)

9600 Wilshire Boulevard
Beverly Hills, CA 90212
(1) 310 275 4211
www.saksfifthavenue.com
@saks

There are a variety of opportunities to find affordable couture when
things go on sale at Saks Fifth Avenue. Watch for their annual
"Friends and Family" 20-percent-off sale, online-only sales and check
out the SAKSFIRST Membership program, which provides privileges,
preferred services and points that lead to gift cards.

Saks Fifth Avenue OFF 5th (SD)

http://off5th.com
@saksOFF5TH

Off 5th has 60 stores in 23 of the United States, offering substantial
discounts on the designer brands sold at the parent store, Saks Fifth
Avenue. A 'More' membership program provides additional
incentives, perks and discounts. Two locations are about an hour
outside of the city at the Camarillo and Desert Hills Premium Outlet
Malls.

Saks Fifth Avenue OFF 5th (SD)

Camarillo Premium Outlet
740 E. Ventura Boulevard, Suite 1400
Camarillo, CA 93010
(1) 805 987 4475

Saks Fifth Avenue OFF 5th (SD)

Desert Hills Premium Outlet
48400 Seminole Drive, Suite 306
Cabazon, CA 92230
(1) 951 849 8415

New York City

New York City needs no introduction, as it is the heartbeat of the American fashion industry as well as a star destination on the retail stage of international fashion. The greatest wealth and nascent creativity resides in Manhattan. The number of stylish customers concentrated in Manhattan buying the best of the best supplies the thriving resale and vintage businesses here. So many designer resale shops carry a carefully culled, but limited, selection of vintage that they should be included on any vintage hunt. Since new merchandise is added daily, these shops should be regular stops on your quality wardrobe-building mission. Each location prides itself on having a knowledgeable and accommodating staff. The plethora of charity thrift stores adds to the wonderful choices, as a thrift store in Manhattan often contains treasures given by wealthy donors.

Designer resale and vintage

BIS Designer Resale (DR)
1134 Madison Avenue
New York, NY 10028
(1) 212 396 2760
www.Bis-Designer-Resale
contact@bisbiz.com

This refined and cozy consignment shop houses shoes, purses, suits, separates and more, all from the most desirable Blahnik, Vuitton, Pucci, Marc Jacobs, Gucci, etc. It is so carefully edited that shopping there feels like an enjoyable treasure hunt in a retail boutique. BIS prices up to 90 percent off retail prices.

(Left) BIS Designer Resale
(Above) Designer Resale

Designer Resale (DR)
324 E. 81st Street
New York, NY 10028
(1) 212 734 3639
designerresaleconsignment.com

Designer Resale, founded by Myrna Skoller, specializes in women's designer clothing and accessories. Since 1990 it has grown from one shop to six brownstone storefronts next door to each other, testament to the high quality of stylish offerings, often referred to by clients as the "Miracle on 81st Street." The Gentlemen's Resale shop opened in 1992, maintaining its position as the only exclusively men's consignment shop.

Encore (DR)
1132 Madison Avenue, 2nd Floor
New York, NY 10028
(1) 212 879 2850
www.encoreresale.com
encore1nyc@aol.com

Madison Avenue is lined with designer retail showrooms. While walking up or down the street, make sure to look UP to the 2nd floor window where you will see Encore (since 1954), a haven for the finest in new and gently worn designer clothing, accessories, and shoes. If you are looking for contemporary Chanel, Hermès, Gucci, Prada, Miu Miu, Marni, Balenciaga and more, you will find it! Special vintage finds also appear on the racks.

Housing Works Thrift Shop – Chelsea (DR & V)
143 West 17th Street
New York, NY 10011
(1) 212 366 0820

Housing Works Thrift Shop – Gramercy (DR & V)
157 E. 23rd Street
New York, NY 10010
(1) 212 529 5955
www.housingworks.org

These thrift shops really are upscale, as generous donors contribute stylish clothing and accessories (and more) to benefit Housing Works, an AIDS social service organization. Besides a separate bookstore café, the "Fashion for Action" one-day event gathers 150 brands for a great experience of shopping and giving. Visit housingworks.org/locations/category/thrift-shops for ten more thrift shops in Manhattan and Brooklyn.

INA (DR)
www.inanyc.com

INA NoHo (DR)
15 Bleecker Street
New York, NY 10012
(1) 212 228 8511
inanoho@inanyc.com

INA SoHo (DR)
101 Thompson Street
New York, NY 10012
(1) 212 941 4757
inasoho@inanyc.com

INA NoLita (DR)
21 Prince Street
New York, NY 10012
(1) 212 334 9048
inanolita@inanyc.com

INA Uptown Women (DR)
208 E. 73rd Street
New York, NY 10021
(1) 212 249 0014
inauptown@inanyc.com

INA Women

Ina Bernstein founded the first INA store in 1993, and this stylish enclave of the finest designer clothing, accessories and shoes has grown into five must-see locations. The Prince Street store solely houses men's designer resale and the Bleecker Street store carries both. It is obvious Ina has been in the fashion business for over three decades, as recognized greats and rare new designers hang together, culled from showrooms, limited editions collections, or runway shoots. To really round out your wardrobe, INA has launched its own label.

La Boutique (DR)
1045 Madison Avenue, 2nd Floor
New York, NY 10021
(1) 212 517 8099
www.laboutiqueresale.com
jon@laboutiqueresale.com

La Boutique (DR)
803 Lexington Avenue, 2nd Floor
New York, NY 10065
(1) 212 588 8898

La Boutique (DR)
227 E. 81st Street
New York, NY 10028
(1) 212 988 8188

La Boutique, a mainstay on the Upper East Side, has been in business for over 15 years. Their broad inventory of the eternal classics – Chanel, Hermès, Dior and others hang graciously with Dries Van Noten, Stella McCartney, Chloé, Vivienne Westwood and Miyake, to name a few. Be sure to visit the second floor.

M.A.D. Vintage Couture & Designer Resale (DR)
167 E. 87th Street
(1) 212 427 4333
info@madvintagecouture.com
madvintagecouture.com

Artful pieces featured at the gallery-like setting include Geoffrey Beene, Valentino, Dries Van Noten, Badgley Mischka, Chanel and more. The shop opened in 2005, with finely curated pieces selected by this former New York art dealer. Her background in fine art, fashion and management have blissfully come together in this beautiful shop.

Michael's (DR)
1041 Madison Avenue
New York, NY 10075
(1) 212 737 7273
www.michaelsconsignment.com
www.facebook.com/century21stores

The consignment shop for women where YSL, Kors, Louboutin, Prada, Chanel and more are sold at 65 percent off retail. Since 1954, this multi-generational family has had resale in their blood. Currently founder Michael Kosofsky's daughter and granddaughter run this high-end bastion of style. You've got to love his philosophy that "every woman can – and should – look like a million without spending a million."

Michael's

New York City Opera Thrift Shop (V & DR)
222 East 23rd Street
New York, NY 10010
(1) 212 684 5344
www.nycopera.com/thriftshop
thriftshop@nycOpera.com

October's Fall Vintage, February's Spring Preview and June's Divas Shop for Opera events only enhance the already wonderful selection of vintage and fine designer finds. Don't let the word "thrift" misguide, as high-end vintage and couture clothing, contemporary fashion and accessories are extremely well priced. Located in stylish Gramercy, this two-level boutique generates proceeds for the creation of costumes for NYC Opera at Lincoln Center.

New York City Opera Thrift Shop

New York City Vintage (V)
117 W. 25th Street
New York, NY 10001
(1) 212 647 1107
newyorkvintage.com
info@newyorkvintage.com

Entering this amazing Chelsea showroom is like stepping back in time. One can get a visual education in fashion history, and the shop has provided inspiration for designers and stylists alike. A 5,000 square foot archive houses their private collection that is available for rental only, with viewing by appointment. When searching for an iconic personality piece for your wardrobe, this is the stop for education and inspiration.

Resurrection New York (DR & V)
217 Mott Street
New York, NY 10012
(1) 212 625 1374
www.resurrectionvintage.com

Katy Rodriguez and Mark Haddawy founded this fashionable vintage resale store in 1996. Katy is a designer in her own right. The prices can be in investment-range, but their two-day flash sales ease the pocket book.

Screaming Mimi's (V)

382 Lafayette Street
New York, NY 10003
(1) 212 677 6464
screamingmimis.com
sales@screamingmimis.com

This emporium of creativity is just the place to add spice to your wardrobe, whether a great coat, purse, statement jewelry piece or dress. Opened in the 1970s by Laura Wills and Biff Chandler, it is a

Screaming Mimi's

New York institution, made famous by its entertainment clientele. It specializes in the 1950s through the 1990s. Wills staffs the store with stylists, so a fashion education is had while browsing. For investment pieces, there is a private penthouse of special finds. Their eBay store and online site allows for round-the-clock shopping.

Second Time Around aka STA (DR)
New York, NY + 11 states
www.secondtimearound.net
www.facebook.com/pages/Second-Time-Around-111-Thompson
@STAconsignment

Second Time Around, aka STA, certainly lives up to its slogan: "Resale Gone Upscale". STA is a premium consignment company that has grown to 25 boutiques in 11 states over its 35-plus year history. Each store is stocked with both new and mint condition resale fashions. They understand the demographics of each neighborhood so it's interesting to visit multiple Manhattan stores on your designer treasure hunt. STA has gained national prominence with its Bravo TV series "Fashion Hunters," exposing the world of resale to the masses.

Lexington (DR)
1040 Lexington Avenue
New York, NY 10021
(1) 212 628 0980

Thompson (DR)
111 Thompson Street
New York, NY 10012
(1) 212 925 3919

Mott (DR)
262 Mott Street
New York, NY 10012
(1) 212 666 3500

Broadway (DR)
2624 Broadway
New York, NY 10025
(1) 212 666 3500

7th Avenue (DR)
94 7th Avenue
New York, NY 10011
(1) 212 255 9455

Sloan-Kettering Cancer Research Center Thrift Shop (DR & V)
1440 Third Avenue
New York, NY 10028
(1) 212 235 1250
mskcc.convio.net/communities_thrift_shop

Known to New Yorkers as the "Bergdorf's of Thrift Stores," Sloan-Kettering Cancer Research Center Thrift Shop is much more than a thrift shop. Here charity meets style, and beautiful Tory Burch, Gucci, Herrera and Valentino can be had for affordable prices, meanwhile helping to bring in over a million dollars a year to the Center. The dedicated volunteer organization also holds the annual Fall Opening Sale held each August, as well the spring and year-end holiday season events.

Sloan-Kettering Cancer
Research Center Thrift Shop

What Goes Around Comes Around (DR & V)
351 West Broadway
New York, NY 10013
(1) 212 343 1225
www.whatgoesaroundnyc.com

It is obvious when entering What Goes Around Comes Around (WGACA) that the owners love clothes. Co-founders Gerard Malone and Seth Weisser are true collectors, amassing thousands of vintage pieces over more than 17 years. Entering their store on West Broadway is like walking into another era where the pieces form a 10000-square-foot archive.

Specialty discount and specialty

Century 21 (SD)
22 Cortland Street #A
New York, NY 10007-3117
(1) 212 227 9092
www.c21stores.com

For fifty years and counting, Century 21 has been the shopping
destination for dedicated shoppers seeking high-end designer brands,
from Dolce & Gabbana, Comme des Garçons, Gaultier, and more for
up to 65 percent off. Century 21 has earned the top ranking for off-
price NYC stores from Zagat! Plans to expand the flagship store with
a café and more shopping amenities will only add to the exhilarating
experience.

Loehmann's (SD)
101 Seventh Avenue
New York, NY 10011
(1) 212 352 0856
www.loehmanns.com
@Loehmanns

Loehmann's (SD)
2101 Broadway
New York, NY 10023
(1) 212 882 9990

Loehmann's carries new, off-price quality designer and name brand
goods priced seriously below retail and is definitely worth a visit. The
Back Room carries high-end designer fashion from international
designers such as Dolce & Gabbana, Calvin Klein, and Donna Karan
to name but a few.

Berlin

Berlin, a hypermodern and ultra-efficient city, is attracting a diverse population, thusly creating a vibrant cultural scene. This European powerhouse has a relative newcomer to their retail scene, often dubbed "first-class secondhand." These are really resale or consignment shops with prices for used top designer garments priced much lower than their counterparts in other European cities.

Vintage and designer resale

Berliner Modeinstitut (V & DR)
Samariterstrasse 31
Friedrichshain, 10247 Berlin
(49) 30 420 190 88
www.berliner-modeinstitut.de

This secondhand store carries mostly vintage pieces, with some designer resale found on occasion, so definitely worth a look.

Das Neue Schwarz (V & DR)
Mulackstrasse 37
Mitte, Berlin
(49) 30 278 744 67
www.dasneueschwarz.de

Das Neue Schwarz, on one of Berlin's important fashion streets, has an inventory of shoes, bags and exclusive vintage designer and new vintage from Vivienne Westwood, Raf Simons, Bernhard Willhelm and Martin Margiela. An online shopping site also makes it easy to check out interesting new finds.

Garments (V & DR)
Linienstrasse 204-205
Mitte, 10119 Berlin
(49) 30 284 777 81
www.garments-vintage.de

The clothing for sale at Garments is separated according to mood, color, and style. There's an exclusive womenswear selection with some excellent merchandise – the sequins section may make your eyes dazzle. A wide range of costumes and dresses for special occasions are also available here. The prices range from bargain to investment.

Humana (V & DR)
Frankfurter Tor 3
Friedrichshain, 10243 Berlin
(49) 30 422 201
www.humana-second-hand.de

Located by the Zoo, Humana sells gently worn clothing at astonishingly good prices. Furs, boots and shoes, purses, countless sweaters and plenty of menswear is on show, starting at €3-7 ($4-9/£2-5) and €50-60 ($64-76/£34-41) for a faux fur or leather jacket in great shape. With a little imagination applied, one could emerge from this shop looking very bohemian-chic from head to toe.

Humana

Kankangou-Mode – Antiquariat & Kulturcafe (V & DR)
Grünberger Strasse 90
Friedrichshain, 10245 Berlin
(49) 52 289 421 93
kultur@kankangou.de

This store/café combo carries 1970s to 1990s thru to current secondhand men and women's garments at affordable prices.

Secondo (DR)
Mommsenstrasse 61
10627 Berlin
(49) 30 881 22 91
www.secondoberlin.de

Secondo has the motto, "First class secondhand," as do many secondhand designer resale shops in Berlin. This particular shop seems to take the motto to heart. The shop is stocked with many secondhand designer labels. New shipments are constantly arriving so it is worth checking more than once.

XVII (V)
Steinstrasse 17
Mitte, 10119 Berlin
(49) 30 544 82 882
www.XVII-store.com

This Mitte area shop is not to be missed. They have everything: from crazy Thierry Mugler vintage avant-garde chic to items seemingly plucked from grandma's attic. XVII is a personal, unconventional fairytale vintage closet scattered with candles and old flea market furniture. Look for beautiful 70s dresses, gothic-style 80s leather, and 60s-era oriental-style items reminiscent of Karl Lagerfeld and Yves Saint Laurent's Marrakech periods.

Sing Blackbird (V)
Sanderstrasse 11,
Kreuzkölln, 12047 Berlin
www.singblackbird.com

This little boutique is in the heart of the newly hip area known as
Kreuzkölln, which is located at the border between Kreuzberg and
Neukölln along one of the canals of the river Spree. Sing Blackbird
combines the pleasures of vintage shopping with a small café. Many
of the pieces in the store are designer pieces, so the price range
fluctuates accordingly. The shop also organizes a monthly flea market,
as well as classic movie screenings and concerts.

Trash-Schick (V)
Wühlischstrasse 31
Friedrichshain, 10245 Berlin
(49) 30 200 535 26
www.trashschick.de

This Friedrichshain shop has a punk attitude reminiscent of the
Eastern block of the 1980s with excellent designer finds.

Specialty discount and specialty

Designer Outlet Berlin (SD)
Alter Spandauer Weg 1
14641 Wustermark OT Elstal
(49) 33 234 90 40
www.designer-outlet-berlin.de

Take the free bus shuttle between the train station Elstal and the
Designer Outlet Berlin. Once there you will find over 100 international
brands and exclusive designer labels in 80 stores. The choice ranges
from CK Jeans, Marc O'Polo and Tommy Hilfiger, to Miss Sixty,
Strenesse and St. Emile. Outlet stores are open Monday through
Saturday, but some open on Sundays during the holiday season.

Flea markets

In German "flea market" is either *"Flohmarkt"* (literal translation) or *"Trödelmarkt"* (junk market). Berlin's best-known and classiest outdoor market is less thrift-sale junk and more antique furniture, jewelry, and clothes. There are special stalls stocked with Burberry and Polo and an eclectic array of designer labels. As with all flea markets, it is always "hit or miss" and requires patience.

Flea Market Arkonaplatz (V & DR)
Arkonaplatz
10435 Berlin
www.troedelmarkt-arkonaplatz.de
Opening hours: Sunday 10am - 5pm; in winter until 4pm

Located in Berlin's trendy Mitte, this flea market is popular with the young and alternative crowd. Here you can find an unusual range of clothing from the 1960s and 1970s. Come in the morning for bargains, as the market's clientele are not early risers.

Flohmarkt am Mauerpark
Bernauer Strasse 63-64
www.mauerparkmarkt.de
Opening hours: Sundays only, 8am - 6pm

A newcomer to the ranks of Berlin's flea markets, this one is located immediately next to the Wall Park (Mauerpark) in Prenzlauer and has maintained a local feel.

Hallentrödelmarkt Treptow (indoor flea market)
Eichenstrasse 4
12435 Berlin
www.arena-berlin.de

Opening hours: Saturday and Sunday 10am - 5pm
Located in a vast former bus depot, not far from the former Berlin
Wall near Kreuzberg, this is the place to go for everything and
anything. Take time to look, as there are plenty of bargains.

Flea Market at Gesundbrunnen Station
Badstrasse
13357 Berlin
(49) 30 383 070 44
Opening hours: Sundays only 7am - 4pm

This flea market is a newcomer to the Berlin Flea Market scene.
Mostly secondhand items where occasionally a bargain can be found.

Berlin Flea Markets

London

London, the very name evokes images of vintage clothing. With a rich and royal past to pilfer from, London's designer resale shops – or dress agencies – have everything for the fashion-obsessed. Some things just get better with age. Charity shops may house some unexpected surprises, as may the multitude of outlets and flea markets, which make shopping a treasure hunt.

Vintage and designer resale

The Dresser (V & DR)
10 Porchester Place
Westminster, London W2 2BS
www.dresseronline.co.uk
thedresser@mac.com
@TheDresser1
(44) 020 7724 7212

This established dress agency has been in Connaught Village since 1986. Stylist Sally Ormsby has her hand on the closet door-handle of London's fashion editors and style makers. As a result, there's a dazzling mix of contemporary and vintage designer labels from Yohji Yamamoto to Yves Saint Laurent. The store's forte is fashion from the 80s.

The Dresser

Designer Sales UK (DSUK) (DR)
Chelsea Old Town Hall, Kings Road, Kensington & Chelsea,
London SW3 5EE
(44) 01273 858 464
www.designersales.co.uk

DSUK, established in 1989, sets up sample sales around London and
the UK. For a £1 ($1.50/€1.20) admission, entrance into the sale
preview hour (12noon - 1pm) gives you access to Vivienne Westwood,
John Galliano, Martin Margiela, Jil Sander, Allegra Hicks, Ralph
Lauren, Etro and more. DSUK sells one-off pieces as well as stocked
items. They work directly with fashion designers in order to offer such
discounted pieces, some of which are for prototypes never put into
production. You now can purchase such amazing stock wherever you
live – in the UK and worldwide – online in the comfort of you're own
home.

The Loft (DR)
35 Monmouth Street
London, WC2H 9DD
(44) 020 7240 3807
www.the-loft.co.uk

The Loft is a unique shop in Covent Garden, buying and selling new
and secondhand designer clothes and accessories for men and
women. Labels such as Gucci, Prada, Vivienne Westwood, Paul Smith,
Chanel, Missoni, Fendi, Marc Jacobs, Dolce & Gabbana, Chloé, Louis
Vuitton, Alexander McQueen, Clements Ribeiro, Jimmy Choo and
more – all at a fraction of the original price. Many items have only
been used on fashion shoots or catwalks; some are samples never
worn. With deliveries arriving daily, repeat visits are necessary.

Octavia Foundation (DR)
211 Brompton Road
South Kensington, London, SW3 2EJ
(44) 020 7581 7987
www.octaviafoundation.org.uk/shops

Octavia Foundation is a non-profit organization dedicated to improving the quality of life for the disadvantaged. For over 20 years, they have filled the South Kensington store with the cast-offs from wealthy patrons who live nearby. Organized by color and category, the store has a designer section including Chanel, Burberry, Hussein Chalayan, Armani, Gucci and Chanel among the regulars. Hermès and other luxury leather goods are on view in a locked cabinet. Downstairs houses vintage books.

Pandora (DR)
16-22 Cheval Place
Knightsbridge, London SW7 1ES
www.pandoradressagency.com

Pandora

In the heart of Knightsbridge Pandora is packed with pre-owned designer labels at a fraction of their original price. At Pandora you will find everything from ball gowns to handbags, from Chanel suits to Jimmy Choo shoes, Moschino Jackets to Valentino cocktail dresses.

Rellik (V & DR)
8 Golborne Road
North Kensington, London W10 5NW
(44) 020 8962 0089
www.relliklondon.co.uk
clairestansfield@relliklondon.co.uk

Rellik sits across from Trellick Tower in North Kensington. Owners
Fiona Stuart, Claire Stansfield and Steve Philip started out 12 years

Rellik

ago in the Portobello Market. Today Rellik's focus
shifts from year to year, with an evolving emphasis
on various designers from the 1960s through the
1990s. Japanese designers and, more recently,
Azzedine Alaïa and Courrèges have been featured.
The most stylish shop here, and ample size ranges
abound. Their annual sale in January is a must to
start the New Year fashionably.

William Vintage (V)
2 Marylebone Street
Paddington, London W1G 5JQ
Hours: By appointment
www.williamvintage.com
@WilliamVintage

William Banks-Blaney opened William Vintage, in 2010. It is a discreet
shop based in fashionable Marylebone. Two floors of wearable vintage
ranging from 1960s day shifts to the finest red carpet, including one-
of-a-kind pieces from Balmain, Balenciaga, Jean Dessès and Madame
Grès. They have a sizable collection of Courrèges and Dior haute
couture. Prices run from £200-4000 ($320-6500/€250-4500), in a
range of sizes. The store is open by appointment only and contact is
by email only.

Specialty discount and specialty

Bicester Village (SD)
50 Pingle Drive
Bicester Village, Oxfordshire OX26 6WD
(44) 01869 323200
@bicestervillage
http://www.bicestervillage.com

Bicester Village, located in Oxfordshire – an hour's drive outside of London – is an upscale outlet collective carrying major designer labels at discounted prices. A complimentary visit with your very own style consultant is available for first-time visitors. You'll find Alexander McQueen, Armani, Céline, Dolce & Gabbana, as well as Valentino, Vivienne Westwood and Yves Saint Laurent. Check out their website to ensure you take advantage of all the other perks this chic, concierge-style outlet has to offer.

Browns Labels for Less (SD)
50 South Molton Street
London, W1K 5SB
(44) 020 7514 0052
labelsforless@brownsfashion.com

Browns Labels for Less, the designer label outlet store with permanently discounted prices, sits across the street from legendary Browns – the iconic retailer founded in 1970 by Joan and Sidney Burstein. Browns is credited with introducing Alexander McQueen, Comme des Garçons, John Galliano and Hussein Chalayan to the retail world, and bringing Donna Karan and Ralph Lauren to the UK. The outlet targets the sophisticated shopper who desires the original and unique – at up to 70 percent off!

Harrods (S)
87-135 Brompton Road
Knightsbridge, London, SW1X 7XL
(44) 020 7730 1234
@HarrodsofLondon
www.harrods.com

This internationally famous store, with a million square feet filled with the best that money can buy, throws two big sales every year. With discounts of up to 75 percent off coveted couture and designer clothes, it is the time to update your acquisition list. The online store has seasonal reductions.

Harvey Nichols (S)
109-125 Knightsbridge
Knightsbridge, London SW1X 7RJ
(44) 020 7235 5000
contactknightsbridge@harveynichols.com
@Harvey_Nichols

The name Harvey Nichols has been synonymous with labels of luxury since 1880, and has maintained its prestigious cadre of classic and cutting-edge designers in the most fashionable London shopping district. Its annual sale is renowned, with up to 70 percent off Missoni, Vivienne Westwood, Lanvin and Alexander McQueen.

Milan

Just the mention of Milan conjures up visions of the catwalk and a chorus of designer names like Armani, Dolce & Gabbana, Gucci, Missoni, Prada, Valentino and Versace. For the followers of fashion, Milan is shorthand for outlet shopping with discounted designer outlets galore. There's even an outlet on the famed Via Montenapoleone, the Rodeo Drive of Milan.

The outlets carry a revolving assortment of last season's looks, including factory seconds and returns. Not all outlets are alike; some are small and crowded, while others have multiple floors. Outlets that aren't run by a brand will have a revolving assortment of designer and couture labels; they can't tell you in advance what they'll have in stock from any particular designer. While Milan's outlets are well known, the regular priced design houses themselves do not promote them. A couple of the outlets are located outside the city center. Armani's Factory Store is an easy half hour drive, whereas Prada's outlet is four hours south.

Global brands and the bigger outlets' websites feature content in several languages. Be prepared to pay with cash at some outlets. It is best to avoid Milan during Fashion Week, held twice a year, in February and September. Remember to ask for a tax-free refund voucher from any boutique with a Global Refund, Tax Refund and Tax Premier shopping sign if you are coming in from outside the European Union. Many shops shut down for part of August so the dates are unpredictable and fluctuate every year. Every outlet is closed during Ferragosto, on August 15th, so be sure to plan in advance. For locations without a website or email address, calling for details is suggested.

> "Outlets that aren't run by a brand will have a revolving assortment of designer and couture labels

Vintage and designer resale

Humana Vintage (V)
Via Cappellari 3
Milan
(39) 02 72080606
www.humanaitalia.org
info@humanaitalia.org

Humana Vintage is operated by Humana People to People Italia, a
non-profit organization dedicated to supporting development
projects in the third world. Humana operates stores in other
European cities. The store focuses on clothing from the 1960s,
1970s and 1980s and includes secondhand finds from Italy's finest
designers: Armani, Dolce & Gabbana, Missoni and Valentino. Note
that the inventory varies dramatically, so this is a store to visit
regularly.

Humana

L'Armadio di Laura (V)
Via Voghera 25, Milan
(39) 02 8360606
www.armadiodilaura.it/armadiodilaura
armadiodilaura@gmail.com

This charming store's motto, "precious things go around and come around," certainly says it all about "Laura's Wardrobe." Located in the Solan neighborhood, inside a courtyard just off the street, this is one of the better vintage shops in Milan. Founded by Laura Gentile some thirty years ago, supported along with way with Adriana Fortin's passion for style, the store is now run by Alice. Here is a place for filling your wardrobe must-haves as well as stylish accent pieces.

Specialty discount and specialty

Armani Factory Outlet (SD)
Strada Provinciale per Bregnano 13
Vertemante
(39) 03 1887373

This is the largest Armani outlet in Europe situated about a half hour north of Milan. This outlet is a gold mine of all the Armani labels, including Giorgio Armani, Armani Collezioni, Armani Jeans, Armani Junior and Armani Casa.

Basement (SD)
Via Senato 15
Centre
(39) 02 76317913

This small shop takes its name from its location, literally down a steep stairway, and not easily noticeable from the street. They only carry size 40 and 42 (sizes 6 and 8 US; 8 and 10 UK). Discounts of 50 to 60 percent off or more on Roberto Cavalli, Moschino, Prada and Dolce & Gabbana, along with up-and-coming contemporary designers.

Dmagazine Outlet (SD)
Via Montenapoleone 26
Via Bigli 4
Via Forcella 13
(39) 02 76006027
www.dmagazine.it

In spite of the famous address, Dmagazine's discounts can be as high as 80 percent. Prada, Miu Miu, Dolce & Gabbana and Gucci are among the many designer labels you're likely to find in this small and somewhat chaotic shop. Dmagazine has two other outlets in Milan. Previous year's inventory can sometimes be found at half off their regular outlet prices.

Dolce & Gabbana Outlet (SD)
Via Rossini 72
Legnano
(39) 03 31545888

The Dolce & Gabbana Outlet is still a bit of a secret. About 20 km (12.5 miles) from Milan, this outlet is very low key: there's only a small sign with the number 72. The outlet carries a wide assortment of goods from their women's, men's, children's and accessory collections at 50 to 60 percent off.

Fidenza Village Outlet (SD)
Via San Michele Campagna
Localita' Chuisua Ferranda
43036 Fidenza (Parma)
(39) 05 2433551
www.fidenzavillage.com

Fidenza Village is about an hour from Milan. Featuring 100 stores
with discounts of up to 70 percent, the hot tickets are Armani,
Bikkembergs, D&G, Escada, Marni, Michael Kors, Missoni, Valentino
and Versace. It doesn't hurt that La Perla and Wolford also have a
presence here. This outlet mall operates a Shopping Express shuttle
that departs daily from the city at Piazza Castello at 10:00 a.m. and
returns at 5:15 p.m. The fare is half-off if booked in advance from their
website. They also provide a free shuttle service to and from the
Fidenza (train) Station – FV, every 40 minutes starting at 9:00 a.m.
Check the website for a schedule.

Prada aka Space (SD)
Via Levanella Becorpi
Localita Levanella
S.S. 69 – 52025 Montevarchi
(39) 05 59789481
www.prada.com/en/store-locator

Space is approximately 400 km (250 miles) from Milan, in
Montevarchi. Located within Prada's manufacturing facility, anything
they manufacture could be in stock at 30 to 70 percent off. The mix
includes both men's and women's ready-to-wear, shoes, perfume,
bags and accessories. There's even a café. Space issues every shopper
with a customer ID upon arrival, streamlining the shopping and
check-out process. It's a first-class experience; they only let up to 100
shoppers in the store at any time. The outlet doesn't close until
8:00pm, but they stop letting people in at 7:30pm.

10 Corso Como Outlet (SD)
Via Tazzoli 3
(39) 02 29015130
shop@10corsocomo.com
www.10corsocomo.com

10 Corso Como is the brainchild of the former editor of *Vogue Italia,*
Carla Sozzani. A five-minute walk from the concept store's flagship,
the cool factor carries over with the assortment of men's and
women's fashion, accessories and shoes by every designer from A to
Z: Alaïa, Ann Demeulemeester, Balenciaga, Céline, Comme des
Garçons, Helmut Lang, Miu Miu, Manolo Blahnik, Prada, Stella
McCartney and YSL. Sozzani favors the color black, so expect to see a
lot of it. Weekly updates to their website list the designer merchandise
in the store. The average discount is 50 percent, with savings of 60 to
70 percent for previous season's designs. If you're buying a lot, don't
hesitate to ask for a discount at the register; often they'll oblige.

(Left) Fidenza
Village, (Below)
10 Corso Como

Paris

Paris, as to be expected, is the center of the fashion universe, both old and new, haute and not. The explosion of designer resale shops in the last decade has presented unlimited shopping possibilities, furthering your chance of looking chic. Divide your shopping trek by *arrondissements* (areas of the city) to effectively manage your time. You are apt to encounter cultural events while shopping, making the experience all the more enriching.

Listed are the vintage, designer resale, fripperies (secondhand), and major department stores offering designer sale merchandise. Sales in French department stores are a tightly regulated event, with two sales seasons – winter and summer. Their starting dates are a matter of administrative decrees and each of the two seasons lasts only six weeks. The winter sales season starts at the end of January and the summer sales begin in late June. The two major department stores in Paris are Le Printemps, built in 1865, and Galeries Lafayette, built in 1893. Designer depots, aka consignment stores, offer designer and couture clothes at deep discounts.

Vintage and designer resale

Alternatives (DR)
18, rue du Roi de Sicile, 75004 Paris
4th arrondissement
(33) 01 42 78 31 50

Most of the inventory is sourced from fashion models, so unique Matsuda, Yohji Yamamoto and Michel Klein are in the mix among the men's suits, women's separates and jackets.

Créatrice De Robes De Rêve (V)
47 Rue d' Orsel, 75018 Paris
18th arrondissement
(33) 01 46 06 80 86
www.zelia.net
zelia@zelia.net

Designer and shop owner Zelia creates every piece in the store. She specializes in one-piece dresses from beautiful vintage fabrics, incorporating deconstructed elements, corsetry, etc. Many could be considered for weddings and special occasion functions. After 30 years, Zelia expresses the very *joie de vivre* in her work.

Dépot Vente de Passy (DR)

14, rue de la tour, 75016 Paris
16th arrondissement
(33) 01 45 20 95 21
www.depot-vente-de-passy.com

This shop specializes in Chanel, Dior, Hermès, Prada, Gucci and more, often at 70 percent off the original price. *Depot Vente de Passy* is a Parisian institution and well worth a visit.

Didier Ludot (V & DR)

24 Galerie Montpensier, 75016 Paris
16th arrondissement
(33) 01 42 96 06 56
www.didierludot.fr
Didier.ludot@wanado.fr

This iconic vintage and consignment shop, run by Didier Ludot, houses the crème de la crème of prêt-à-porter, couture, and one-of-a-kind LBDs. His private collection exhibition of LBDs in Paris (1996) spawned his book *The Little Black Dress: Vintage Treasure* (2001, Assouline). French designers Lanvin, Chanel, Balenciaga, Givenchy, Balmain, YSL, and Hermès are the specialty. The high prices reflect the highest quality of wares, but this shop is well worth a visit to experience museum-quality clothing.

Gavilane (V & DR)
14 rue Malher, 75003 Paris
3rd arrondissement
(33) 01 48 87 73 13
gavilane.creation@wanadoo.fr
www.gavilane.com

Gavilane is an amazing store in the heart of the Marais district.
Owned by singer-designer Aden, Gavilane has a Goth feel, yet is so
much more. Charming and soft-spoken, Aden thinks women should
be able to afford something beautiful. Custom garments with
Victorian lace and jet beading are sensational and the accessories are
outstanding. Do not miss this shop!

L'Habilleur 8 (DR)
44 rue de Poitou, 75003 Paris
3rd arrondissement
(33) 01 48 87 77 12

Located in the fashionable Marais district, this is the place to look for
deals. For women, there's a great selection of designer labels
including Plein Sud, Issey Miyake and Jean Paul Gaultier. Men's suits
from Roberto Collina and Paul & Joe are at slashed prices. New
designer garments are from the prêt-a-porter collections from one or
two seasons past, clearly labeled with season information.

Misentroc – Vavin (DR)
15 rue Vavin, 75006 Paris
6th arrondissement
(33) 01 46 33 03 67

Misentroc (DR)
63 rue Notre Dame des Champs,
75001 Paris
1st arrondissement

Misentroc has two boutiques featuring men's and women's designer
clothing. Misentroc on rue Vavin is more youth-oriented, while the rue
Notre Dame des Champs store is more classic. Ready-to-wear Yves
Saint Laurent along with Agnès B and Hermès scarves can be found,
with an occasional haute couture treasure.

Misentroc

Mouton à Cinq Pattes (DR)
8 rue St. Placide, 75006 Paris
6th arrondissement
(33) 01 42 84 25 11
http://www.moutona5pattes.com

Mouton à Cinq Pattes carries samples and gently or never worn
designer garments, including Jean Paul Gaultier, Moschino, Alberta
Ferretti and more. Combing through each rack is well worth the time.

Odetta (DR & V)
76 rue des Tournelles, 75003 Paris
3rd arrondissement
(33) 01 48 87 08 61
www.odettavintage.com
odetta76@gmail.com

Located near the Place des Vosges, Odetta is one of the few
consignment shops – verging on vintage – open on Sundays! Many
gently worn designer items, Louboutin stilettos and recent creations
from Isabel Marant are among the broad selection.

Priscilla (DR & V)

4 rue Mouton- Duvernet, 75002 Paris
2nd arrondissement
(33) 01 45 39 30 03

Priscilla, the owner, collects such signature names as Yves Saint Laurent, Kenzo, Max Mara, Christian Dior and Sonya Rykiel. You are well advised to take time and search for the treasures.

Réciproque (DR)

New York shopper Nancy Greengrass on a Paris trip to Reciproque

88, 89, 92, 95, & 101 Rue de la Pompe, 75016 Paris
16th arrondissement
(33) 01 47 04 30 28
http://reciproque.fr

Nicole Morel founded Réciproque, the biggest and best-known designer depot for resale merchandise, in 1978. There are four separate shops clustered down the street, divided into seven boutiques specializing in various clothing, coats, shoes, boots, accessories and men's clothing. Note the Chanel room downstairs in the Femme boutique, and don't miss the Hermès, Prada, Thierry Mugler, Issey Miyake, Dior, John Galliano, Gucci and Dolce & Gabbana.

Marches aux Puces de Saint–Ouen (V)
Porte de Clignancourt
Saint-Ouen, 93400 Paris
(33) 6 03 44 95 19
www.marchesauxpuces.fr
Open Saturday to Monday all year

Flea market usually denotes uneven quality of a wide variety of items, with a few finds of vintage housewares. The reality is that it is unlikely that a Christian Dior suit is just lying around, waiting to be discovered amongst the stalls. Much like flea markets around the world, inexpensive goods abound. Individual sales or small enterprises yield better finds. These large events are part carnival, part bazaar, but don't expect to find a Chanel original for €50 somewhere in the over 2000 stalls. It is recommended for a fun junk hunting day, but requires a lot of patience to find any buried treasures.

 TIP

Bring cash and go early in the morning. Plan other boutique shopping in Montmartre. The best day is Sunday. Paris flea markets are open during the week except during certain seasons.

Tokyo

Tokyo is enigmatic, a city with contrasting characteristics and a subway system best described as an underground beehive. Street addresses are written macro to micro, in the following order: state, city, neighborhood, number (refers to a section or block), then the building name, and finally the unit or room number. However, this exciting metropolis has some of the best vintage and designer recycle shops. It is important to note that vintage or designer resale items not sourced in Japan, but overseas, are often too large for the Japanese body, so "remaking" of garments abounds. The popularity of American or European brands is strong, but sizes sold tend to be on the smaller size.

Nakameguro, Harajuku, Dakaiyama, Shimokitazawa and Ebisu are the popular areas for vintage treks. Keep in mind that the merchandising style here in recycle shops is more about mixing and matching old with new, especially blending military gear, sneakers and capes with traditional wares. You may find yourself inspired with new ideas about how to freshen up your outfits. Since the Tokyo vintage buyers regularly source from Europe and America, there is an amazing inventory, making it a fashion education in itself. Whether resale, recycle, used, or vintage, the world is found on the racks! Make sure to check store websites and blogs for updated information, store directions and efficient transportation routes.

Alcatrock Vintage Dress Shop (V)
1F Dear Ebisu Building
1-32-14 Ebisu-Nishi, Shibuya-ku 1F
(81) 03 6427-0909
www.alcatrock.com
www.alcatrock.blogspot.com

Dresses, tops, hats, coats and shoes are available for purchase or rent. This store is organized and categorized, as is their website.

American Rag Cie (V)
5-8-3 Minami Aoyama Minato-ku
(81) 03 5766 8739
http://www.americanragcie.co.jp

American Rag Cie, founded by Mark Werts, began in California and he
has now opened multiple shops in Tokyo. This visionary founder was
one of the first to merchandise up-and-coming new designers and
classic brands with a finely edited mix of vintage – unheard of over 25
years ago. Today the stores, in America and Japan, are still style
leaders.

(Left) Alcatrock
Vintage Dress
Shop, (Below)
American Rag Cie

Antiqulosium (V & DR)
Tokyu Apt. 1F 20-23 Daikanyama-cho Shibuya-ku
Tokyo, Japan 150-0034
(81) 03 3461 5295
www.antiqulosium.com
www.blog.antiqulosium.com

Owner and vintage buyer Kikumi Haneda carries a mix of high quality vintage items, including Halston, Gucci, Diane von Furstenberg, Pucci, and many many more! The deep mix of sunglasses, hats, brooches, jackets, dresses, etc., are beautifully archived, spanning the 20th to 21st century. It is clear that this owner really does "love vintage, love fashion, love life," as stated on her blog – a veritable fashion magazine, inspiration board and wonderful insight into the creative mind of Haneda. Her own vintage-inspired label, "21st Century Flapper," is also worth investigating.

Chicago Jingumae Store (V)
6-31-21 Jingumae Shibuya-ku
(81) 03 3409 5017
www.chicago.co.jp

This secondhand clothing retailer was founded in 1996 and has five stores in Japan, four located in the Tokyo area. They carry Japanese, American and European secondhand clothing for men, women and children, including shoes, hats, purses and more. Collectible items abound, with affordable prices. With an American office in St. Louis, Missouri, and an Ibaraki warehouse in Japan, there is a constant turnover of inventory. A search here will uncover conversation pieces to complement your wardrobe.

Hypnotique (V& DR)
Tokyoldo Bldg 2F 1-13-4, Jinnan, Shibuya-ku
Tokyo, Japan
(81) 03 3770 3906
http://hypnotique.exblog.jp
Hypnotique.tokyo@gmail.com

Hypnotique is close to Tokyo's busiest train station, in the heart of trendy Shibuya. A sign below the store says "Ladies Antique Clothes." Hiding at the top of a flight of stairs, this cute little shop is crammed with colorful objects of desire. All manner of vintage mode can be found, including scores of European designers like Céline, Ferragamo, Yves Saint Laurent, Pucci and Gucci.

(Left)
Antiquolosium,
(Below)
Hypnotique,
(Far Below)
Julio

Julio (V)
2-2-2 B1F, Honcho, Kichijoji, Musashino-shi, 180-0004
(81) 04 2223 1337
www.tippirag.com/shopsyo_julio_kichi#

This used clothing shop is housed in a basement, so look for the "Nakamichi – Shopping Street" sign and you are on your way. There is an ample stock of vintage clothing for men and women, as well as hats, purses, and accessories. This shopping hunt will be great for accent pieces rather than demure classics.

Pass The Baton (V & DR)
Omotesando Hills West B2F 4-12-10
Jingumae Shibuya-ku
Tokyo, Japan
(81) 03 6447 0707
http://www.pass-the-baton.com
omotesando@pass-thew-baton.com

Pass The Baton has two stores in Tokyo, each with a distinct
personality. Both locations are a mash-up of vintage American kitsch
and in-demand designers. The Omotesando Hills store is the
preferred venue, where its exhibition space houses Comme des
Garçons, Nina Ricci, Marni and more. It is worth visiting their online
store, which often has a better selection of these designers since the
store inventory rotates quickly. Omotesando is popularly referred to
as the Champs-Élysées of Tokyo.

Piña Colada Used & Vintage Shop (V)
1-5-10, Kamimeguro, Meguro-ku, Tokyo
www.pinatokyo.com
pinacolada@inatokyo.com

It can be interesting to scan their website; you might spy Vivienne
Westwood shoes, a Karl Lagerfeld skirt, or beautifully hand-painted
1950s skirts from Mexico, 1980s Betsey Johnson, a Marni or See by
Chloé. Visit the store and you will find accessories and other
treasures. The inventory ranges from the 1940s to today.

Rag Tag (V & DR)
3-3-15 Ginza, Chuo-ku, Tokyo
(81) 03 3535 4100
http://www.ragtag.jp
http://www.ragtag.jp/english/index.html
@RAGTAGonline
1-17-7 Jinnan, Shibuya-ku, Tokyo
(81) 03 3476 6848

(Left Above)
Pass the Baton
(Left) Piña
Colada (Above)
Rag Tag

Rag Tag has been selling vintage threads for over 25 years. You'll find Louis Vuitton leather goods and clothing, Hermès, Vivienne Westwood, Alexander McQueen, Martin Margiela, Lanvin, Dries Van Noten, Alexander Wang, Comme des Garçons, Yohji Yamamoto and Manolo Blahnik. The men's selection is equally impressive. Rag Tag has five stores in Tokyo. The two biggest are on the Ginza, with seven floors, and the Shibuya location that has four. Many of the 100 employees in the Ginza shop are multilingual. Rag Tag has a membership program called the R Card and, by spending 100000 JPY ($1195/£760/€915), they'll give you a discount of 1500 JPY ($18/£11.40/€14).

Screaming Mimi's (V)
18-4 Daikanyama-Cho, Shibuya Ku
(81) 03 780 4415

This haven of quality vintage originated in New York City in the 1970s.
Owner Lara Wills' Tokyo branch brings together the styles of Pucci
and Yves Saint Laurent with quirky period pieces, for an eclectic
inventory. The spice for your wardrobe will be found here, as well as
some beautiful statement-making garments to supplement your
classics.

Specialty discount and specialty

Premium Outlets (SD)
There are three outlets outside of Tokyo housing the top designer and
basic brands. Visiting each website ensures added savings, including
online coupon vouchers and a detailed sale calendar to further
enhance your savings.

Gotemba Premium Outlets (SD)
1312 Fukasawa
Gotemba-Shi, Shizuoka, Japan
(81) 0412 0023
www.premiumoutlets.co.jp/en/gotemba

Everything about Gotemba is big. Mt. Fuji makes a majestic backdrop
for the big name brands that claim considerable real estate at this
center. The store directory reads more like the lineup for Fashion
Week: Alexander McQueen, Armani, Balenciaga, Barneys New York,
Bulgari, Blumarine, Chloé, Cynthia Rowley, Dior, Dolce & Gabbana,
Escada, Etro, Gucci, Issey Miyake, Jil Sander, Jimmy Choo, Paul Smith,
Marni, Salvatore Ferragamo, Valentino, Vivienne Westwood, Tsumori
Chisato, Moschino, Maison Martin Margiela, Yves Saint Laurent, and
more. Depending on what train you take, Gotemba Premium Outlet
Mall is about an hour outside of Tokyo.

Sano Premium Outlet (DD)
#2058, Koena-cho,
Sano-Shi, Tochigi, Japan
(81) 0 327-0822
www.premiumoutlets.co.jp/en/sano

Sano is set in natural surroundings against the backdrop of Mt. Mikamo, but looks like an East Coast town in the US. It houses many famous brands including Courrèges, Hiroko Koshino, Cynthia Rowley, Etro, Escada, Gucci, Kate Spade New York, Krizia, Lanvin, Marc by Marc Jacobs, Michael Kors, MK Michel Klein, Paul Smith, Prada, Ralph Lauren Factory Store, Ferragamo, Theory, Sergio Rossi, Yves Saint Laurent, Banana Republic, Brooks Brothers, Armani Factory Store, Coach and Cole Haan, to name a few. The list alone makes it worth taking the less-than-one-hour train journey from Tokyo!

Ami Premium Outlet
2700 Yoshiwara
Ami-machi, Inashiki-gun, Iabaraki, Japan
(81) 0 300 1155
www.premiumoutlets.co.jp/en/ami

The third of the Premium Outlets to open in the Kanto area, Ami houses more of the classic wardrobe builders including Cole Haan, Brooks Brothers and Ralph Lauren Factory Outlet, as well as plentiful denim and sportswear brands. Travel time is about an hour or so from Tokyo.

Gotemba

Inside the Internet: let your fingers do the shopping

The Internet is the Wild Wild West when it comes to the abundance of online private sales, shopping clubs, sample sales and other member-driven, time-limited flash sales and discount offers on designer and luxury brands. Most of the sites listed use social media like Facebook or Twitter to keep members informed. Look for their blogs, referral programs and VIP perks. Whether it's pre-owned designer handbags or the must-haves from last season's runway, the world of affordable couture is at your fingertips.

The Real Real
www.therealreal.com

The Real Real is US-based and offers pre-owned accessories and clothing up to 90 percent off retail price with 72-hour sales and an ongoing warehouse sale. A general membership is free, the First Look membership is $5/£3/€3.50 a month, and they welcome consignments.

Portero
www.portero.com

Portero sells pre-owned and vintage, authenticated, luxury accessories. An assortment of the finest designer handbags, shoes, jewelry, watches, belts, and pens can be searched by brand. For example, you can narrow down a Louis Vuitton search by price, category, material and color. They welcome consignments. Subscribe to their email newsletter and receive an extra $50/£30/€35 off your first purchase.

Net-a-Porter
www.net-a-porter.com

Net-A-Porter is an online fashion retailer with the look of a fashion magazine that features the latest fashions from every design house known to woman. Their end-of-season sales are the ticket for real bargains. Sign up for a free account to receive their Fashion News. Net-A-Porter ships to 170 countries, and customer service is available in English, French, Spanish, Italian, Dutch and Arabic.

The Outnet
www.outnet.com

The Outnet is the online outlet for *Net-A-Porter*. They host time-limited discount shopping for designer clothes, accessories, shoes and gifts.

Vente-Privee
http://en.vente-privee.com

The matriarch of European online private sales for over 20 years, Vente-Privee is a members-only site offering time-limited sales and covering eight countries: the UK, France, Belgium, Spain, Germany, Austria, Italy and the Netherlands. Each flash sale is focused on one brand and designer discounts can add up to 70 percent off. UK and Dutch members who refer friends can earn vouchers for credit towards their next purchase. This site is chock full of information, including a community forum.

Far Fetch
www.farfetch.com

Far Fetch is an online marketplace featuring designer goods from independent fashion boutiques around the world. Their sale selection is immense, with discounts of 30 to 70 percent off. Look for luxury labels like Alexander McQueen, Ann Demeulemeester, Valentino, John Galliano and Balenciaga. You can shop multiple boutiques in the network with one checkout, and they ship all over the globe. Customer service is available in English, French, Italian, Spanish or Portuguese.

1st Dibs
www.1stdibs.com

1st Dibs is a luxury portal known for its strategic partnerships with 1000 dealers of decorative arts and fashion. The fashion search options let you choose from haute couture, vintage, ephemera and capsule collections by various designers. One-of-a-kind Madame Grès, Gianfranco Ferrè, Mariano Fortuny and Romeo Gigli showed up last time we looked. Customize your haute couture search by price, from low to high, and you might see an original croquis (sketch) of a cocktail dress by Hubert de Givenchy for $300. Once you find something you want, you contact the dealer directly and negotiate a price. For a 20 percent buyer's premium, 1st Dibs can facilitate the negotiation on most items for you.

Cocosa
www.cocosa.com

Cocosa offers steep discounts on various designer labels via time-limited sales only to persons in the UK. They guarantee everything sold on the site is genuine and new. Register to receive daily or weekly alerts.

Designer Sales UK
http://designersales.co.uk

Designer Sales UK is a go-to site to get up-to-the-minute information on the who, what, where and when for sample sales in the UK. Subscribe to their newsletter to receive advance notifications on upcoming designer and retailer sample sales held at three venues in London and Brighton. An online shop offers up to 90 percent off retail prices. Their DSUK VIP Invite program guarantees you get in the door ahead of the queue. Sample sales often feature items from Jil Sander, Armani, Viktor & Rolf, Balenciaga, Vivienne Westwood and Prada. Lalita, a London boutique that specializes in vintage accessories for both men and women, regularly participates in DSUK.

Sample Sales London

www.samplesales.co.uk

Sample Sales London is an online calendar of sample sales from retailers and designers alike. A weekly newsletter keeps subscribers abreast of upcoming sales.

Love Fashion Sales

www.lovefashionsales.com

Love Fashion Sales is a search engine that connects shoppers with 400 UK high-street retailers, designers and e-commerce sites that sell last season's collections. A unique feature of Love Fashion Sales is that it sends you a "sale alert" every time something matched by the brand, product category and size you've specified, goes on sale.

Buy VIP

www.buyvip.com

Enjoy discounts of up to 70 percent off time-limited sales on designer brands with your free membership. Their campaigns, as they call their sales, are available to shoppers in Spain, Italy, Germany, Austria, Portugal, Poland and the Netherlands.

Glamour Sales

Japan
www.glamour-sales.com
China
www.glamour-sales.com.cn

The world of affordable couture is at your fingertips.

Picture credits

Every effort has been made to credit the appropriate copyright holder. Please let us know if there are any misattributions or omissions and they will be corrected in any subsequent printing.

Unless otherwise credited all photographs were taken by the authors, all drawings are © Jemi Armstrong and digital graphics were provided by Wynn Armstrong. P.11 Art Resource, NY © Brooklyn Museum Costume Collection at The Metropolitan Museum of Art. P.13 photograph courtesy of Helene Samson © 2011. P. 15 Art Resource, NY © Brooklyn Museum Costume Collection at The Metropolitan Museum of Art; Gift of the Brooklyn Museum, Gift of Irene Stone. P.17 Art Resource, NY, © The Metropolitan Museum of Art; jacket gift of Mrs. John Chambers Hughes and skirt gift of Christian Dior. P. 22 'Gilda' © 1946, renewed 1973 Columbia Pictures Industries, Inc. All Rights reserved, courtesy of Columbia Pictures. P. 23 photograph Lorrie Ivas. P. 25 Art Resource, NY, © Brooklyn Museum Costume Collection at The Metropolitan Museum of Art; Gift of the Brooklyn Museum; gift of Kay Kerr. Pp. 29, 30 photograph Angelika Sjostrom, courtesy of The Way We Wore. P. 34 from a private collection, drawing © Rene Gruau for Jacques Fath.. P. 44 photograph Linda Arroz and Fernando Escovar. P. 50 photograph Wynn Armstrong. P. 55 © The Estate of William Travilla-Bill Sarris, Giiorgos Dimakis, reproduced courtesy of Art House Licensing. P. 67 © 2011 Maidenform, Inc. P. 69 Fernando Escovar P. 74 photograph courtesy of Rita Watnick and , Micheal Stoyla. P. 78 Superstock Vintage Images; and photograph Lorrie Ivas. P. 86 photograph Lorrie Ivas. Pp. 91, 94, 98 photographs Linda Arroz and Fernando Escovar. P. 99 © Getty Images, Inc. P.100 advertisement from 1947 *Vogue* magazine (author's collection). P.103 Linda Arroz and Fernando Escovar. P. 104 Courtesy of Jiffy Steamer Company, LLC. Pp. 122-125 Pablo Solomon. Pp. 134-135 photographs courtesy of Lady Malpas. Pp. 136-139 photographs courtesy of Deborah Woolf. P. 143 Courtesy of William Vintage. P.147,150-151 Fernando Escovar.

Acknowledgements

Both authors particularly wish to thank Wynn Armstrong and Lorrie Ivas for their generous contributions to the book and everyone at Vivays Publishing especially Lee Ripley and Pierre Toromanoff.

Additional thanks from Jemi Armstrong to the many friends and colleagues who gave of their time and expertise; Elizabeth Mason, Joanne & Brian Stillman, Cheryl Lyles, Nina Sheffield, Lisa Berman, Gina & Sasha Cassevetes, Fereshteh Mobasheri, Liza May Carlin, Marsha Hale, Blackie and Hugh Simmonds. I am grateful to them all. A special personal thanks to my patient husband Wynn Armstrong whose contributions were given with generosity and love

Linda Arroz would also like to thank my dear family, friends and colleagues near and far for their generosity of time and support. Kyrian Corona, Bobette Stott, Joyce Michel, Rita Watnick, Micheal Stoyla, Kris Bruckner, Doris Raymond, Margaret Schell, Rick Ashitani, the L.A.P.D, Danielle Patee, Mai Shimokawa, Elizabeth Mason, Evan W. Miller at the Japan National Tourism Organization, Emanuelle Boni at the Agenzia Nazionale del Turismo, Neil Citron, Michele Rothstein, Chinami Inaishi, Yoko OHara and Linda Tucker from Fashion Group Tokyo and Los Angeles respectively, Louise Coffey-Webb, Janie Bryant, Andrea Berthold-Rupp, Alex Masi, Susanne Friend, Rebecca and Samuel from Tokyo Telehone, Beverly and Pablo Solomon, Susan Dalgliesh, Deborah Woolf, Lady Malpas, Fernando Escovar, and Sho Mikami.

Index